Business Road Warriors

AIRPORTS, AIRPLANES, FACES AND PLACES OF BUSINESS TRAVEL IN THE LATE '80S

Eddie Morgan

Copyright

ISBN-13: 978-1-944662-20-2

Published by Realization Press

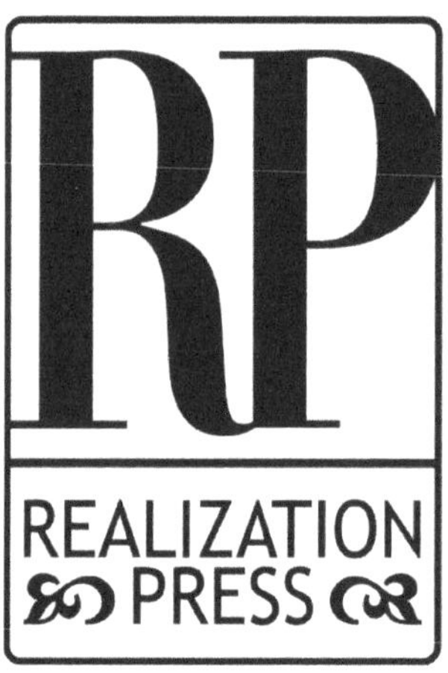

Cover Photo: Eddie Morgan
Cover design: MAS Graphic Arts

Dedication

To the love of my life, my wife Patty

INTRODUCTION

Business Road Warriors is a photo essay of the people, the places and the stories of some of the people encountered during business travel in the late 1980s. It includes images of the crew and fellow travelers (many with their personal stories), as well as the terminals, the equipment, and the support personal required to make it all work.

In the last three decades, the rate of change for our society has increased at an incredible rate as predicted in the 1970s by Alvin Toffler in his best seller, *Future Shock*. Virtually all aspects of our lives have been affected by these increasingly rapid changes.

One aspect that has changed dramatically, is business travel. This change has been driven primarily by advances in communication.

In the late eighties most companies had never heard of a website, and the internet was in its infancy. Vendor/customer relationships were primarily face to face. A vast majority of people did not have cell phones (no one had smart phones) and "text" was a noun, not a verb. Business travel was a fact of life for many industries, as face to face was the preferred way to communicate with customers and prospects.

Business Road Warriors includes images of terminals, equipment, and the workers, who made the system function. It also includes images of crew and passengers, some of whom provided personal stories.

The pilots in this era were undergoing a change, based on the changing technology of the airplanes they flew.

The older planes were basically flown manually by highly skilled pilots. The newer ones contained avionics that were, to a much greater degree, computer controlled. The cockpit of a 727, for example, is dramatically different than that of a 757.

In the 1960's flight attendants were required to be single females with strict rules as to weight, hair length and other requirements. They were unashamedly hired based on their looks and personality.

By the late 1980's, many of these rules were changed. The flight attendants of this era were both male and female, and weight restrictions were reduced or eliminated. Still they were the face of the industry to most passengers. Of course, they each had a story, and some shared those stories in this book.

Some terminals were quite photogenic. They were, in many cases, small cities that never slept, operating twenty four hours a day. The life blood of these cities was an army of workers who handled the baggage and maintained the facilities, but were invisible to the most travelers. These workers, their stories and images are some of the most compelling in the book.

Fellow travelers also provided fascinating vignettes captured in the book. Many shared personal information about themselves. These unsubstantiated comments are sometimes humorous, sometimes sad personal details and dreams of fellow passengers. The personal information volunteered to a stranger on an airplane is amazing.

The images from three decades ago prior to Photoshop® and other post-processing software available today may seem pedestrian to younger viewers. However, these images present an authenticity which to some extent has been lost in the current era.

While we rush headlong into the future, there is a something calming in a nostalgic look into the circumstances that existed three decades ago.

THE PHOTOGRAPHS

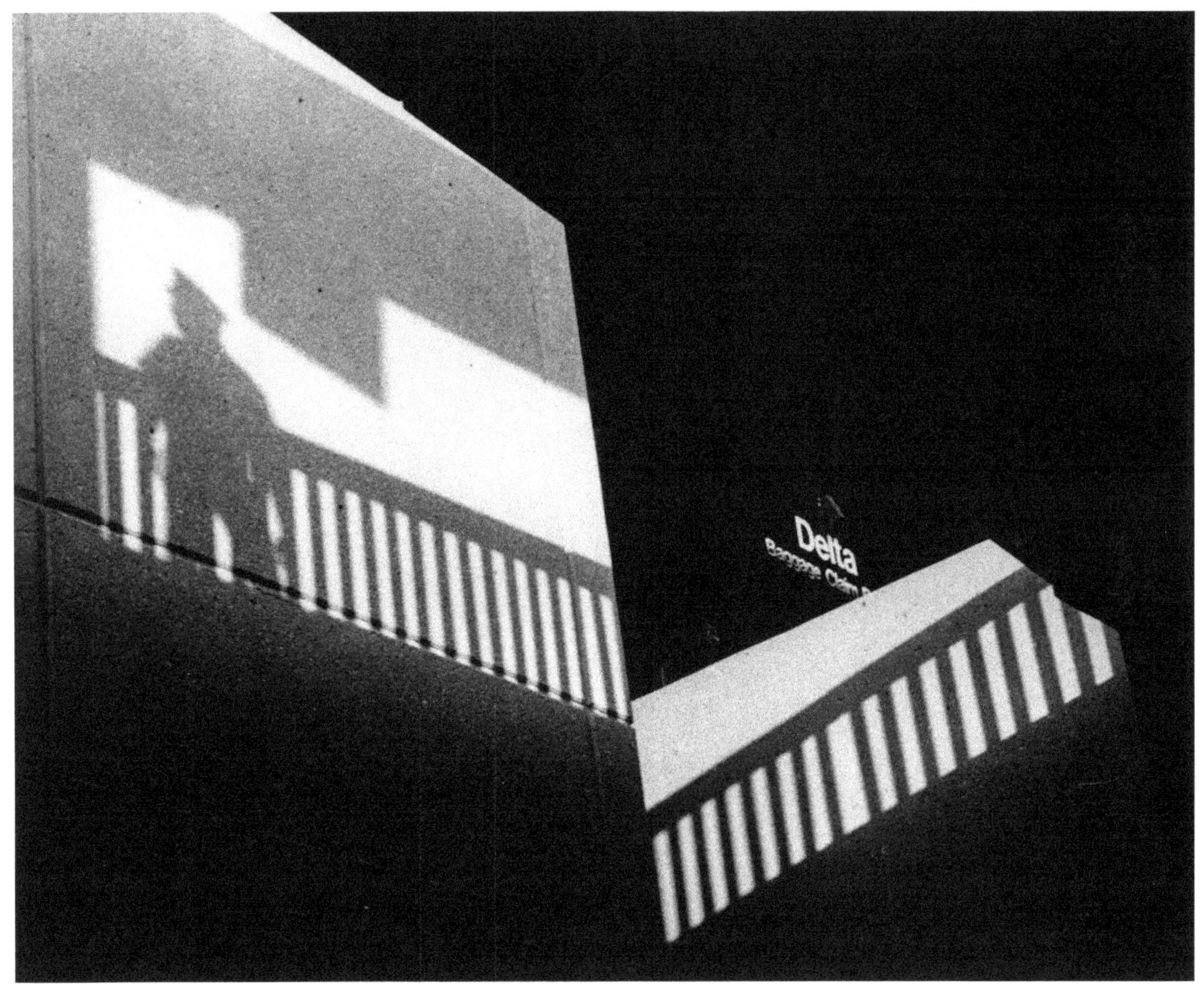

Skycap at Dulles Airport

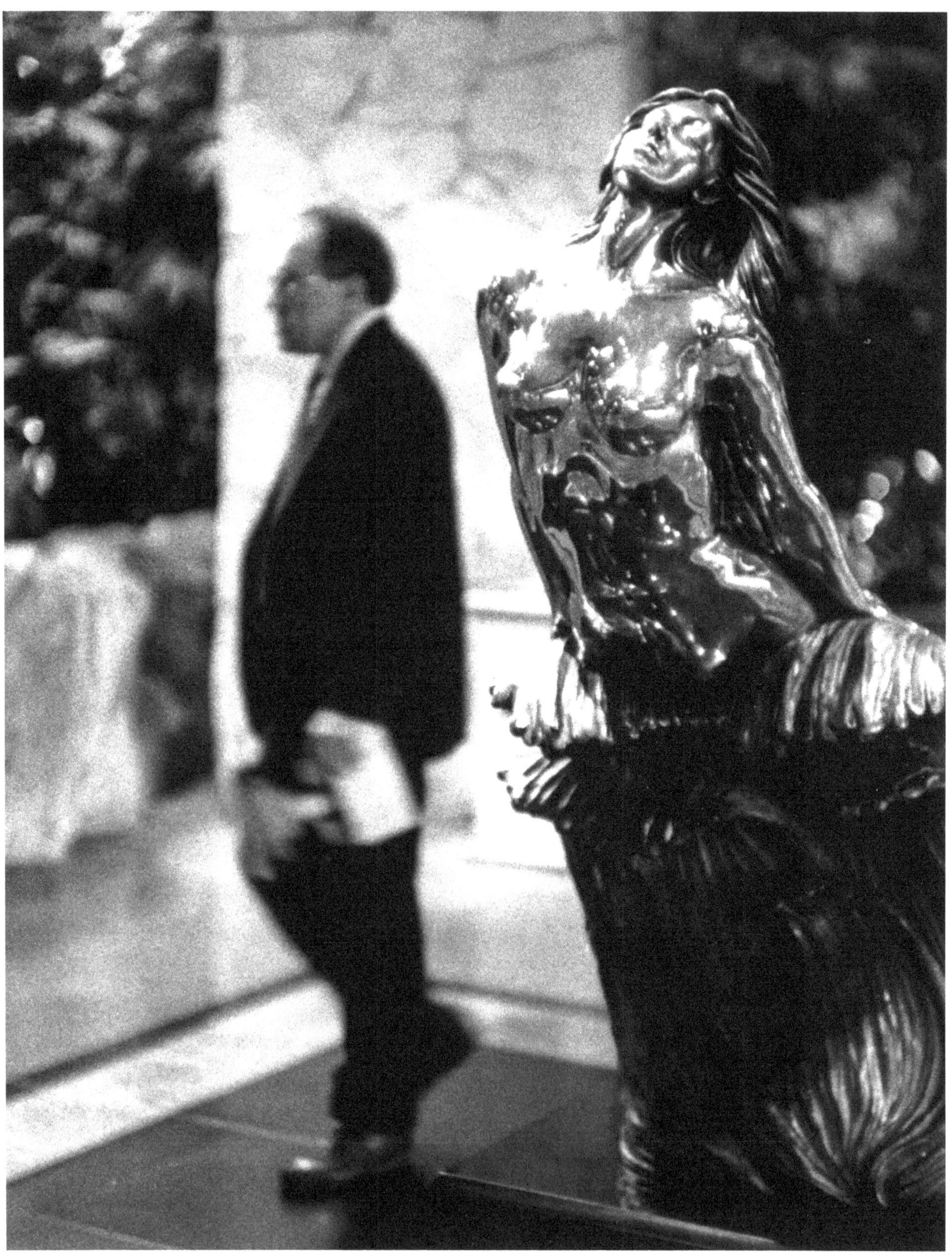

Mirage Mermaid Hotel Lobby

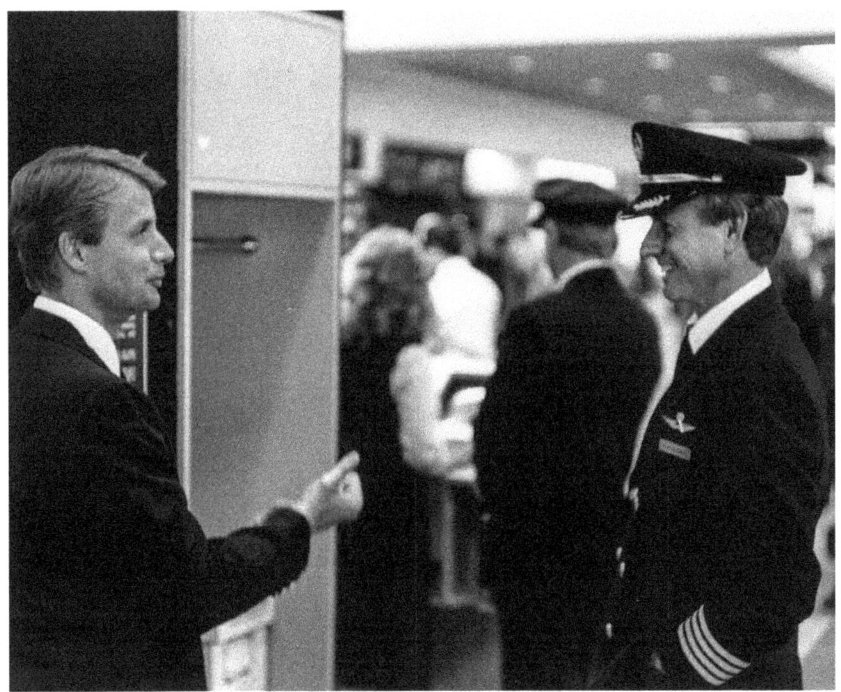

Although pilots were highly paid in some cases, the requirements for pilots were sometmes lowered, depending on the availability of trained military pilots.

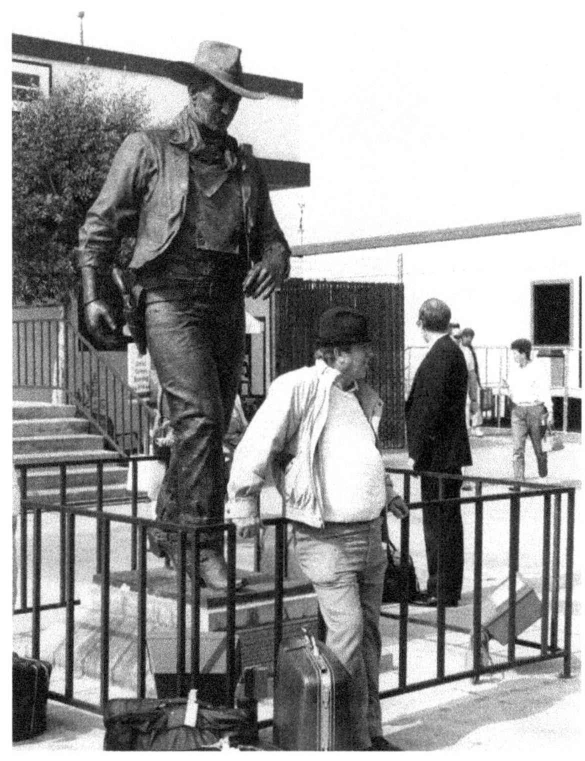

The Duke
John Wayne Airport

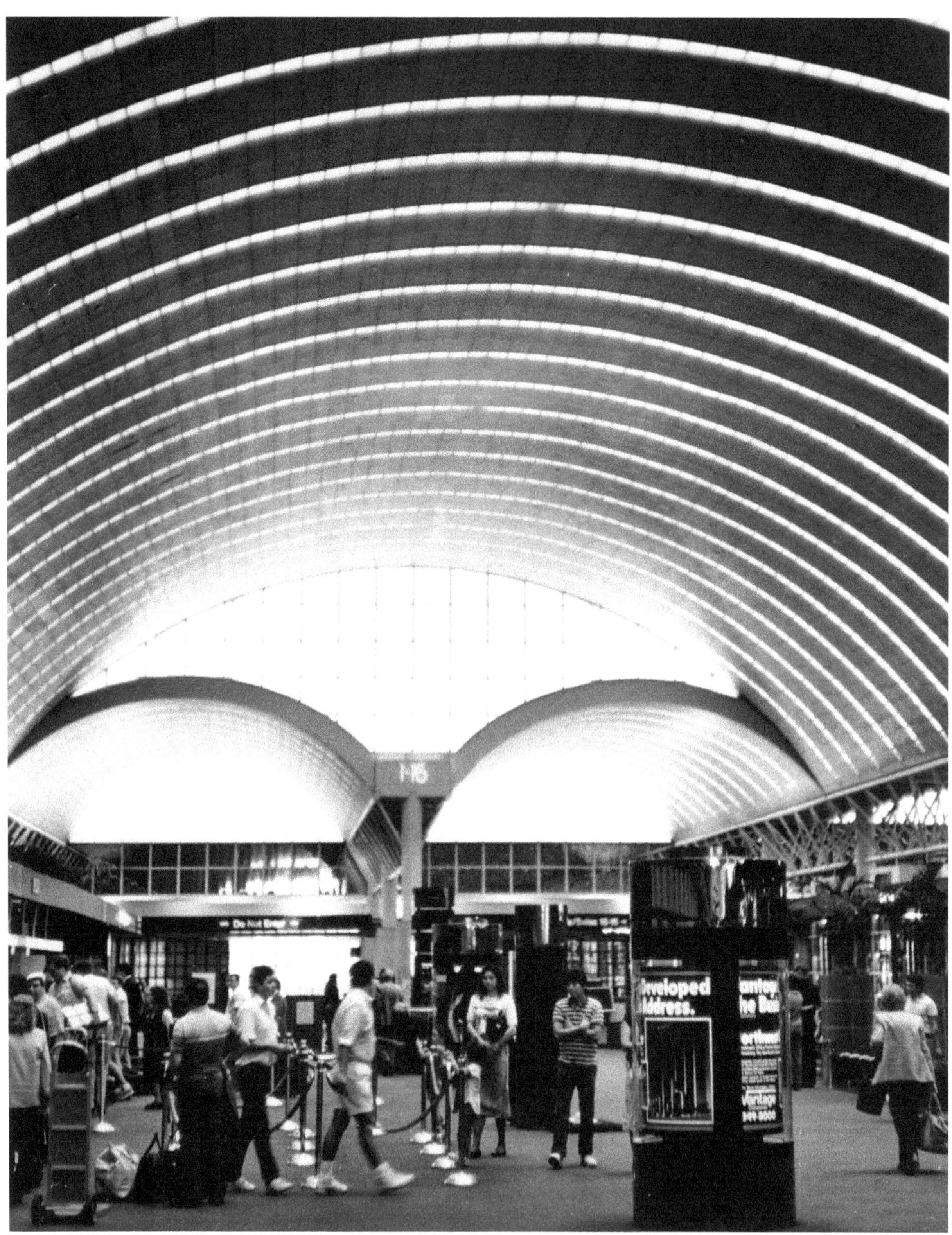

San Antonio Terminal

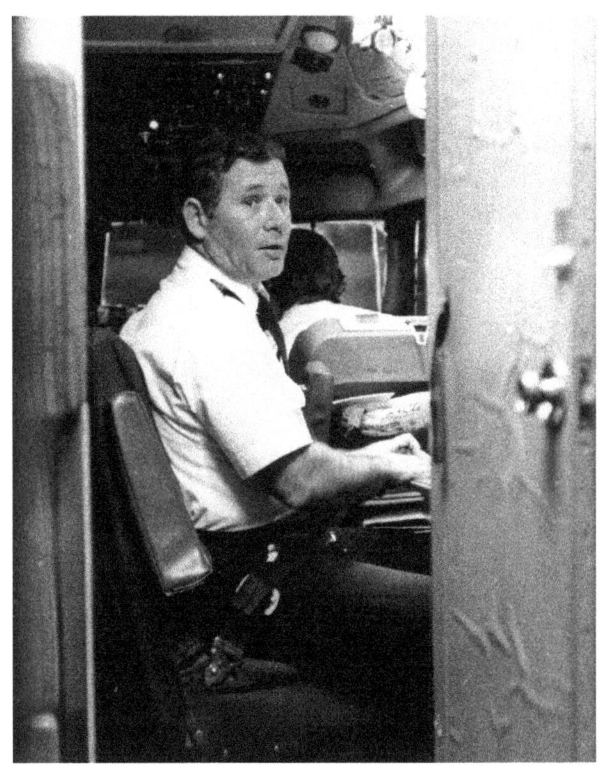

The old 727s, some still in use in the '80s, had a pilot, a co-pilot, and a navigator. The navigator faced the right side of the aircraft rather than the front and this was called riding side-saddle.

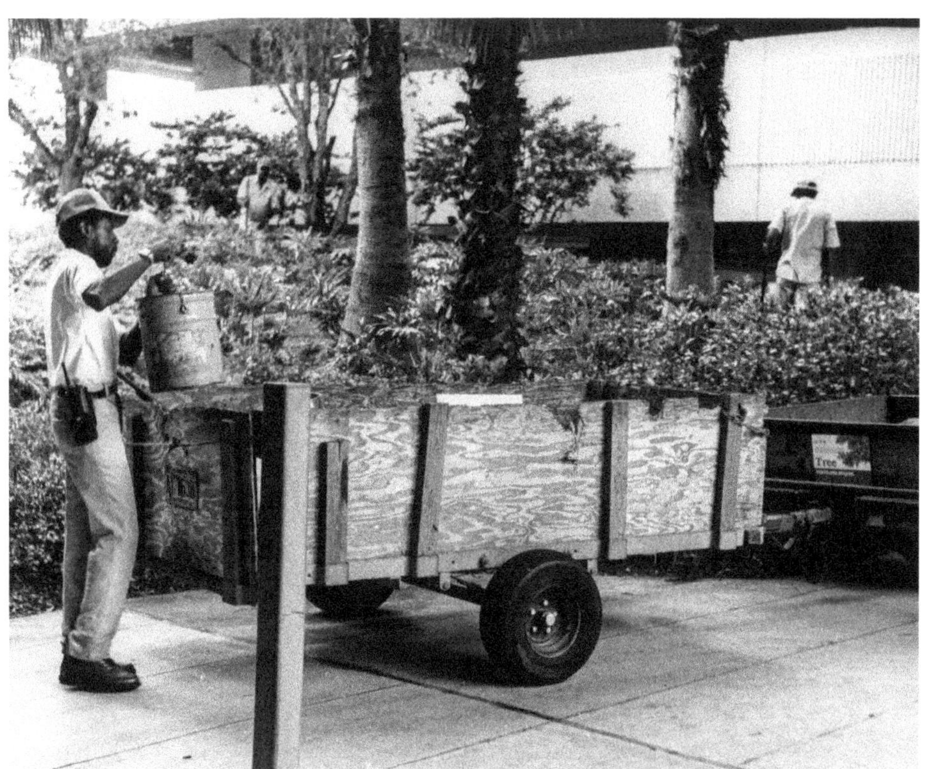

Landscaping crew, Ft. Lauderdale

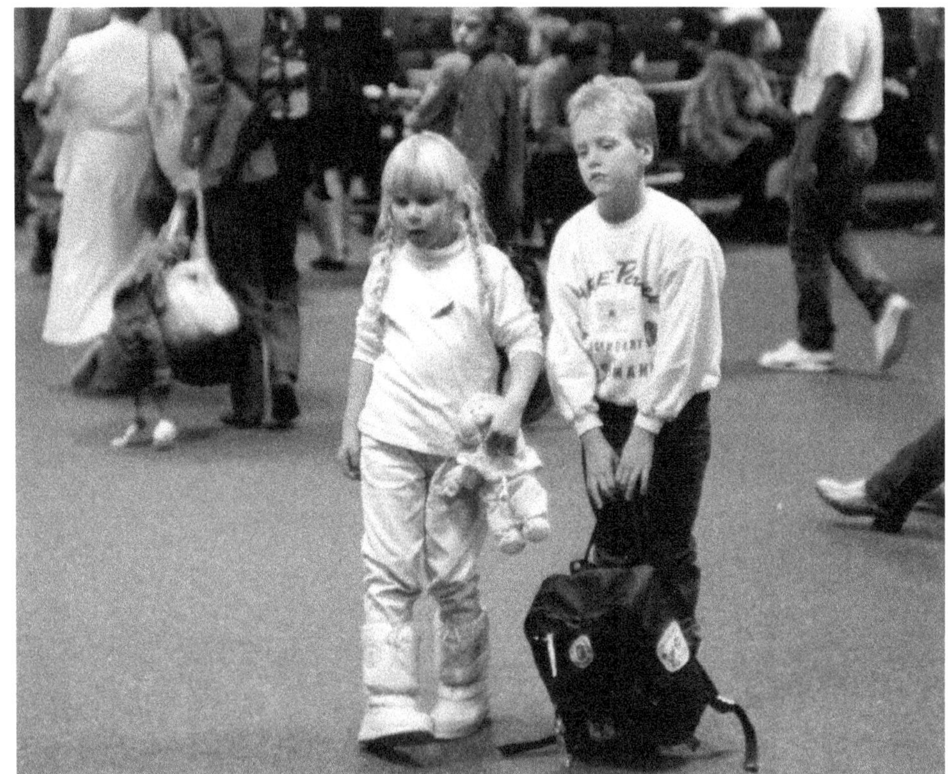

Houston Flight Delay

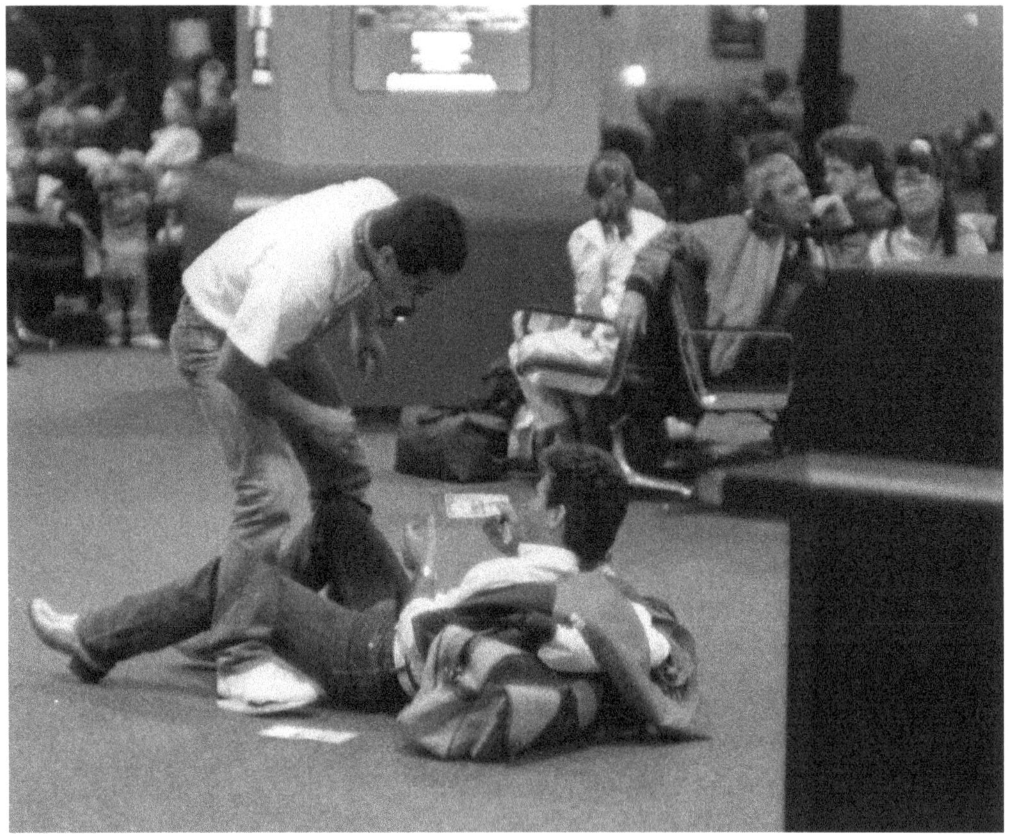

Liar's Poker while waiting for a flight in Houston

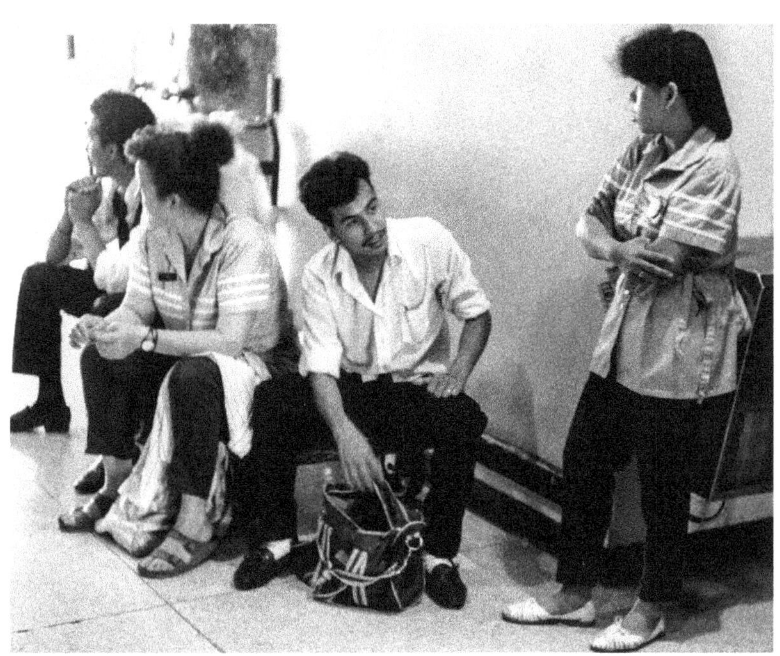

Break
O'Hare, Chicago

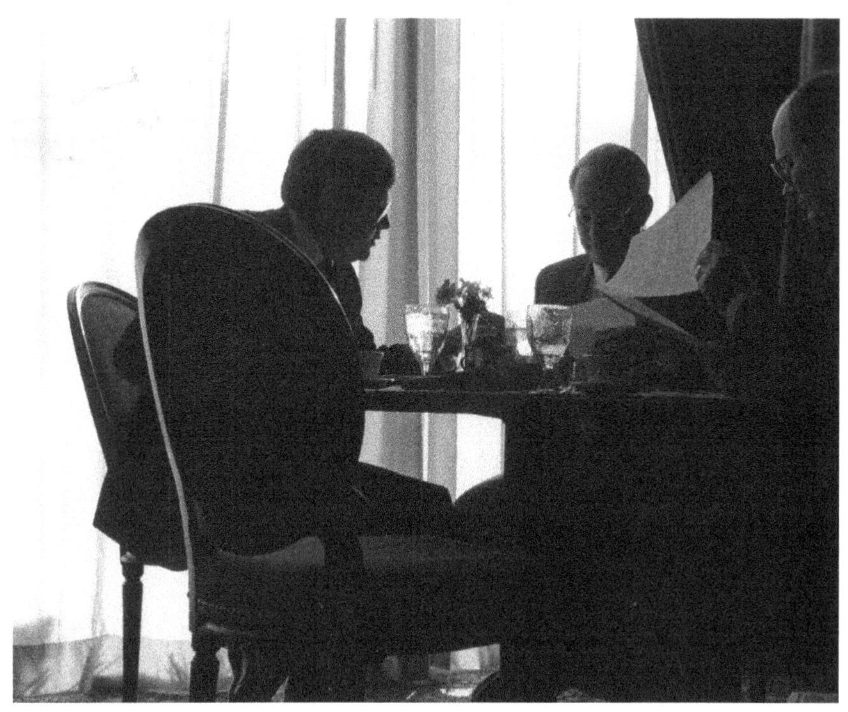

Breakfast Meeting
Houston Holiday Inn

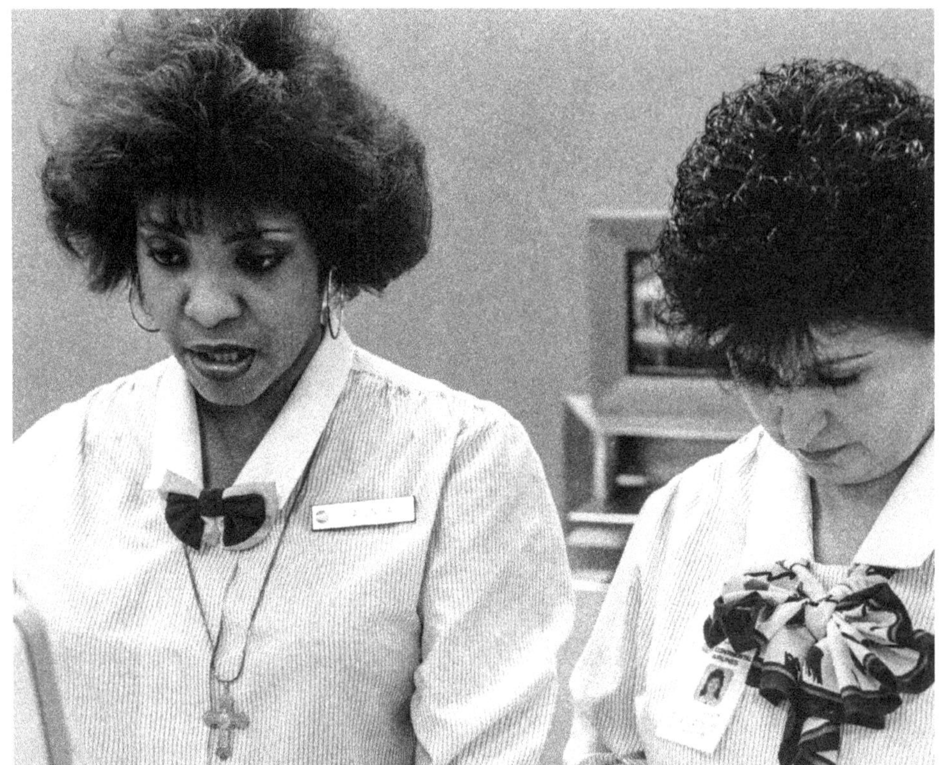

The gate agents, in some respects, have one of the more difficult jobs. Here they are "overriding the system."

She just graduated from Flight Attendant school with Eastern, and was flying to Pittsburgh to start her career in April 1988. After labor disputes and a crippling strike in 1989, Eastern collapsed in 1991. In retrospect, probably bad timing.

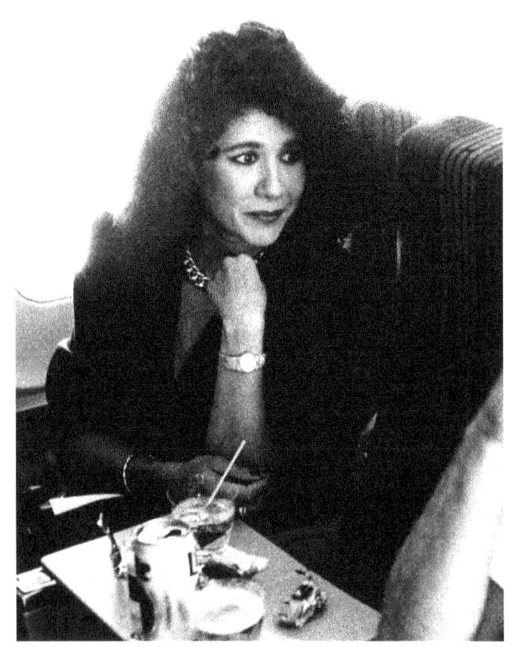

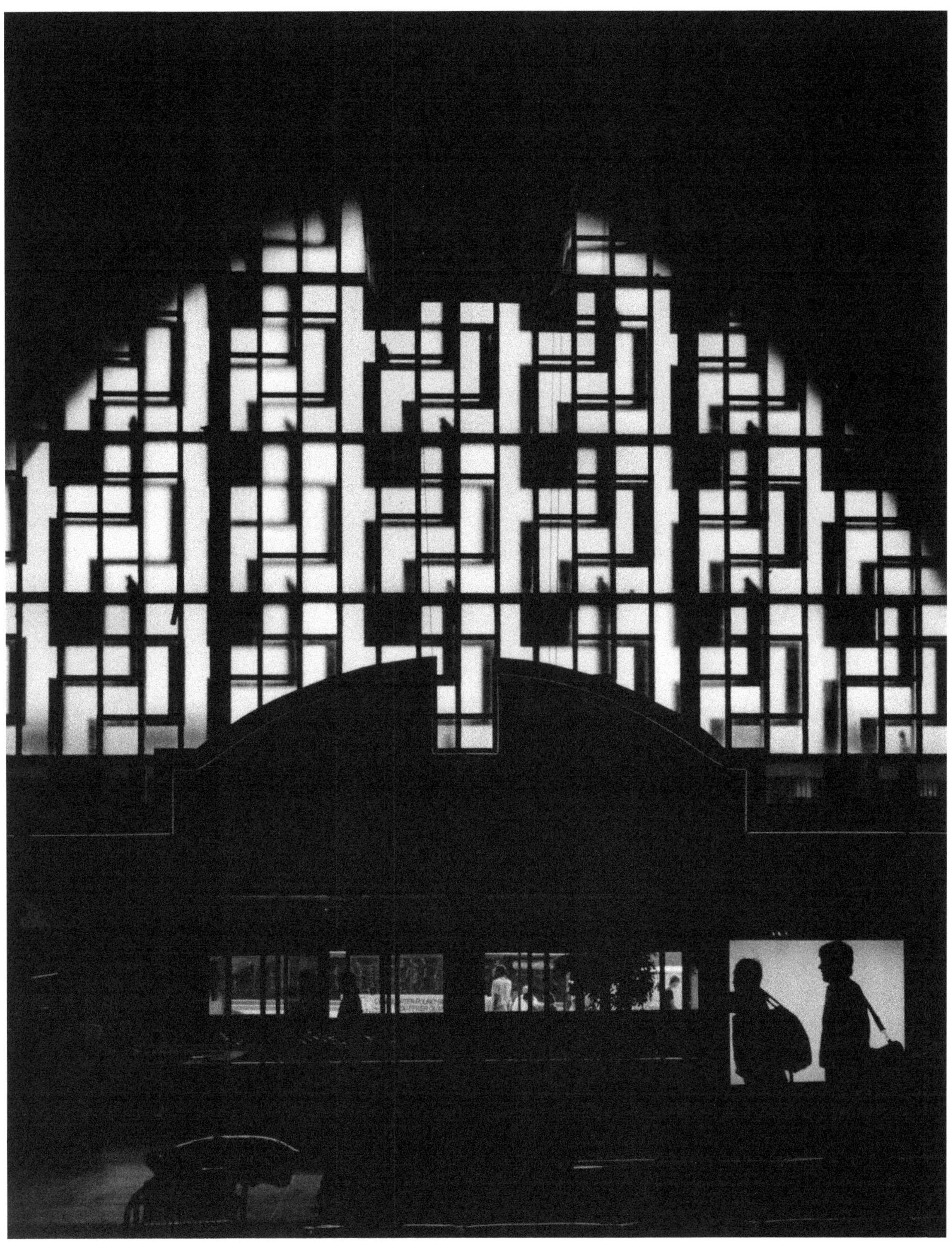

New Orleans Terminal

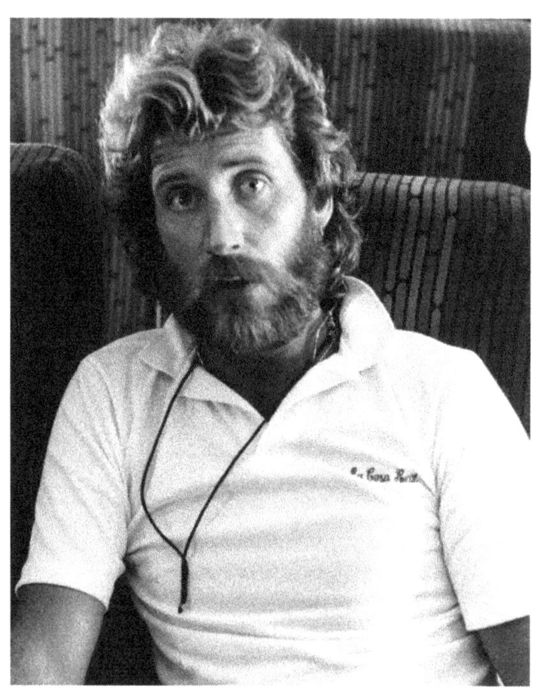

He was a professional crew member on racing yachts. He told me he hoped, one day, to use the MBA he earned at Harvard.

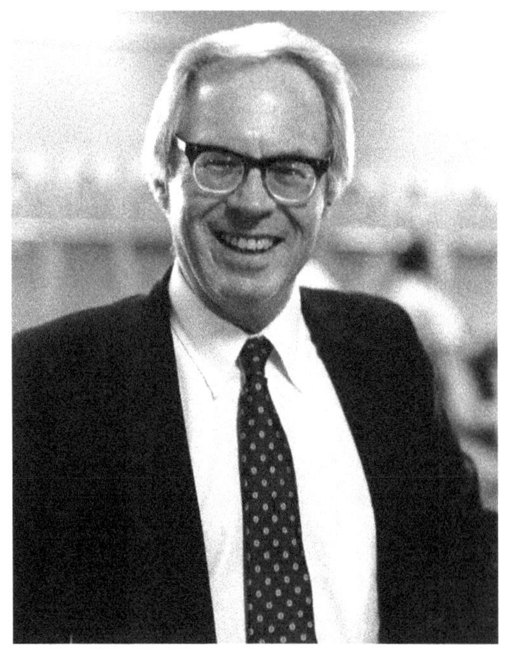

He was a Dean of the Florida Law School. He was currently running the Florida Department of Corrections under a court order due to overcrowding.

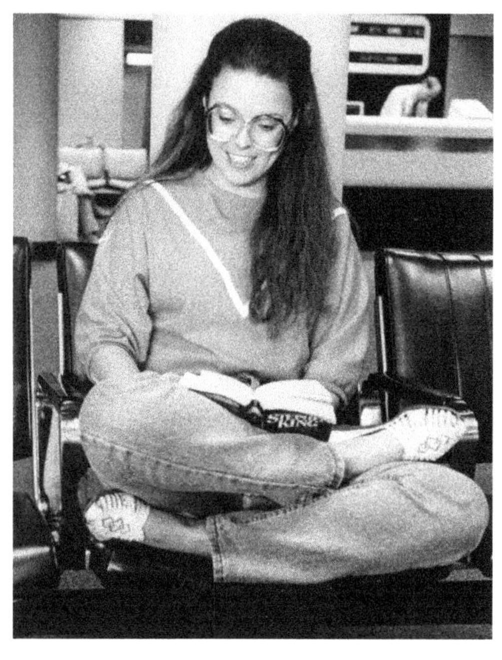

She was beautiful and looked too young to have been a communications consultant for AT&T for 18 years.

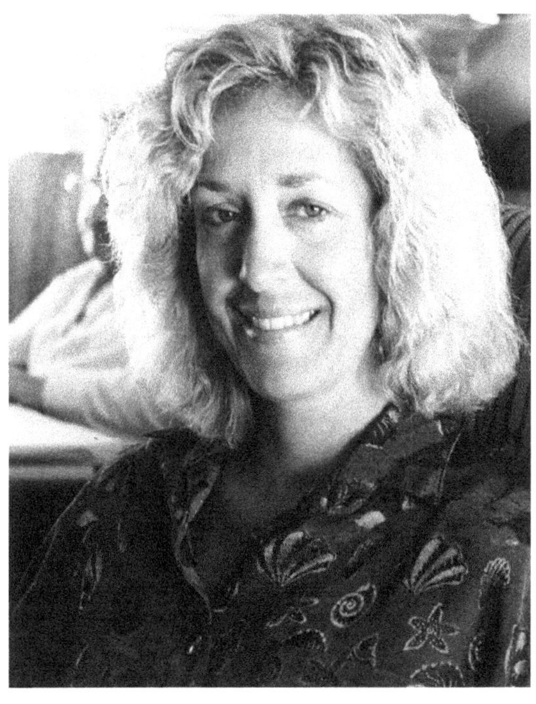

She was a marketing executive for a fast food franchisor. She was married to a TV producer, and this was the second time, by coincidence, I had sat next to her on a flight. She was tired of the corporate grind and someday wanted to teach in a small college.

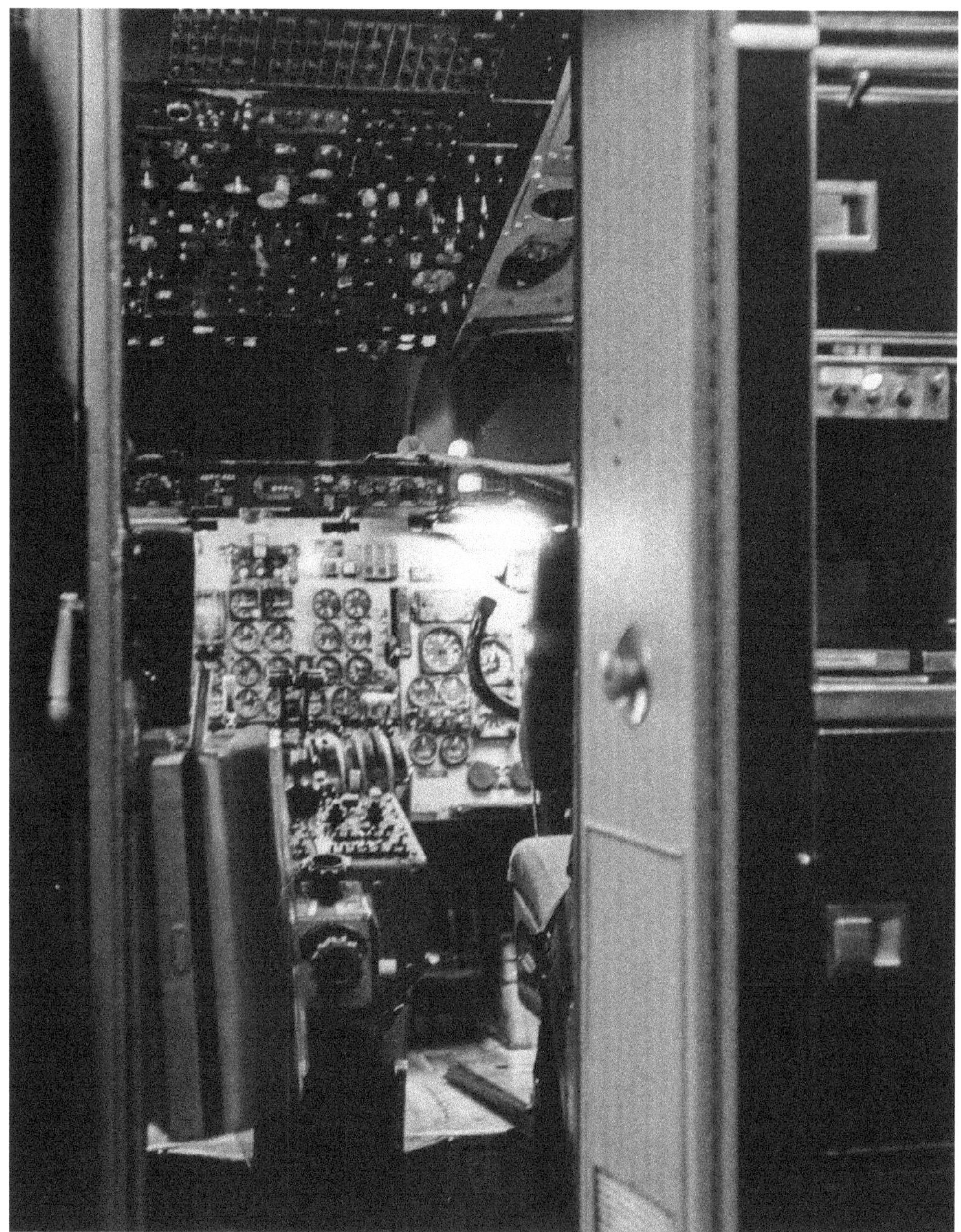

Front Cabin DC-9. Airplanes Avionics (the instruments used to fly the aircraft) were changing rapidly in the late '80s. The DC-9, a predecessor to the MD-80, had the older instruments and depended more on the pilot. A pilot for an L-1011 during this period, bragged that he could set the controls in Atlanta and not touch them until after landing in Los Angeles. Even allowing for hyperbole, this was a major advance, and probably considered "crude" by today's standards.

Eastern emergency exit

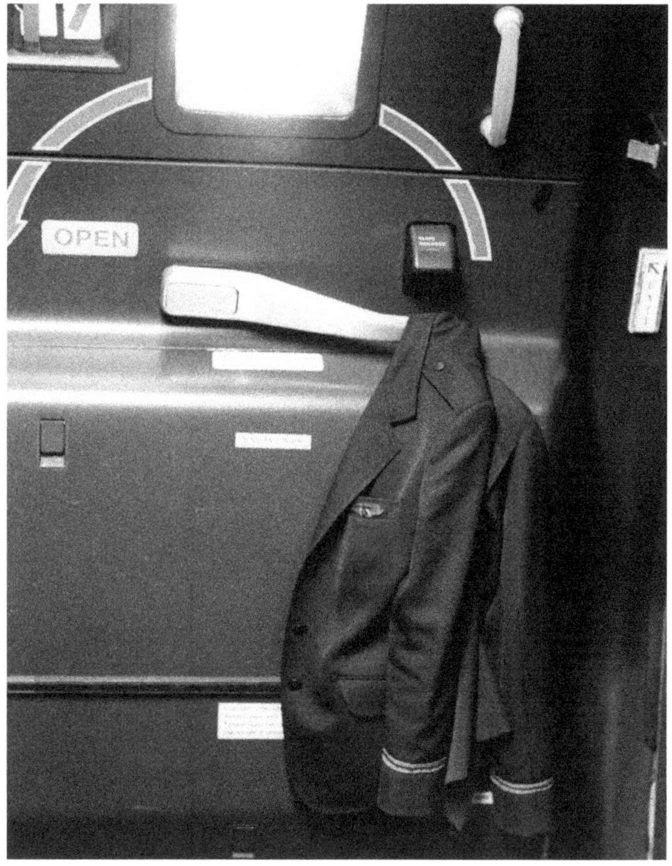

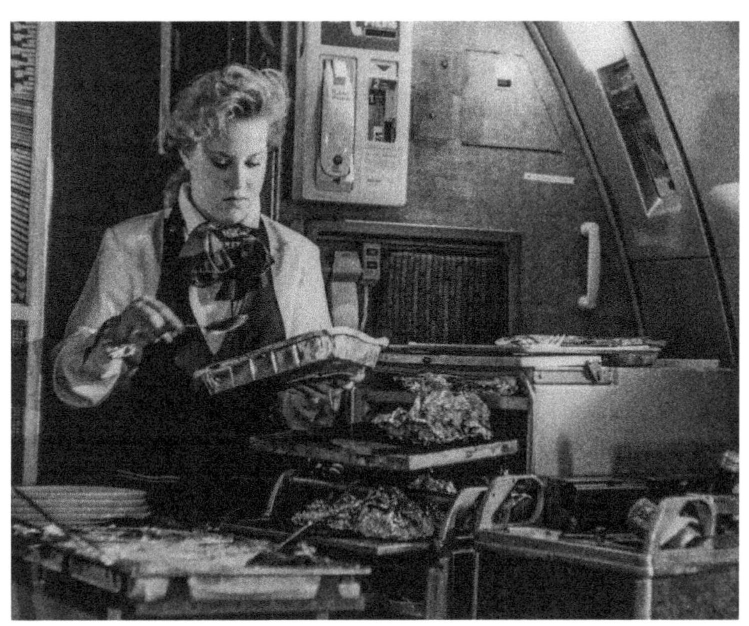

Food Service:
The most work a Flight
Attendent does is food and
beverage service.
Los Angeles to Atlanta

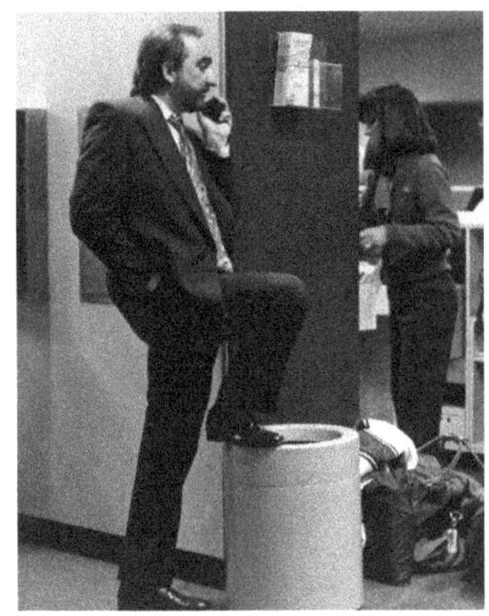

Cool phone
Atlanta

Relaxing in the I-Club

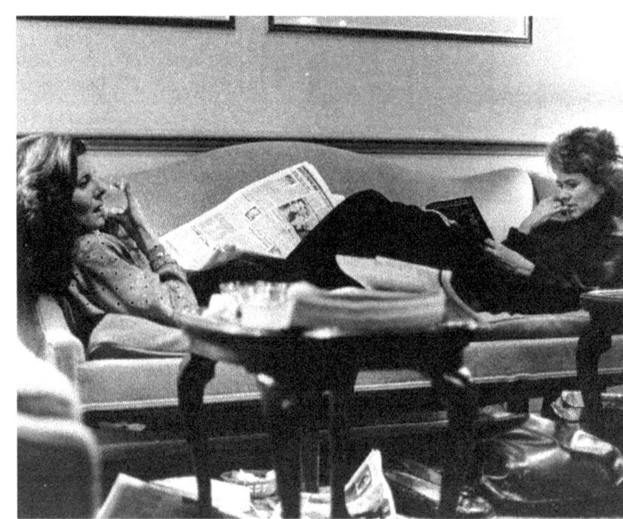

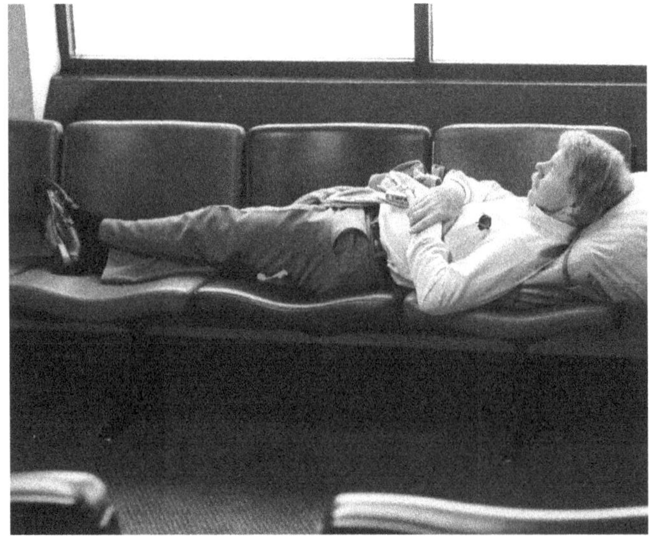

Nap Time
Houston Hobby

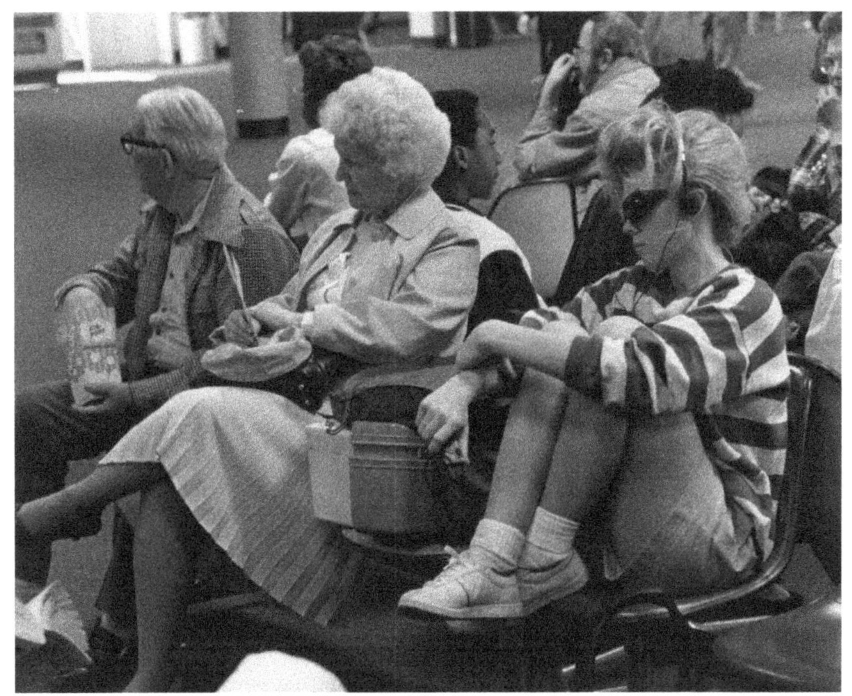

Generation Gap
Atlanta

Bag Claim
Orange County, CA

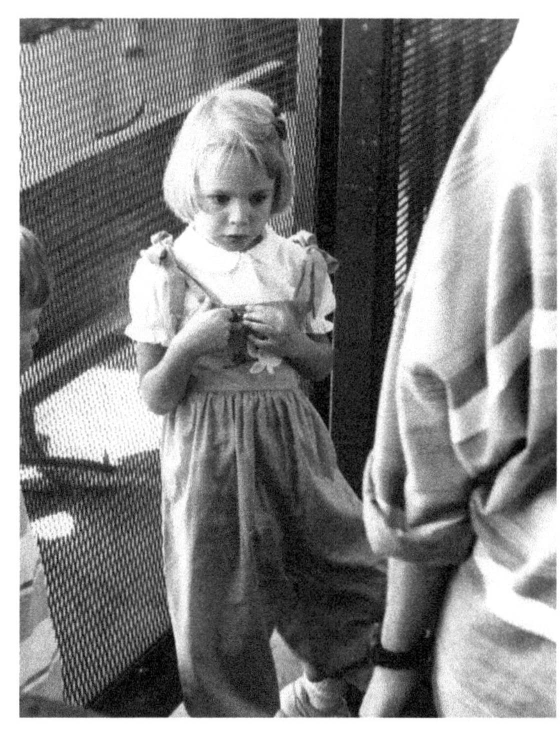

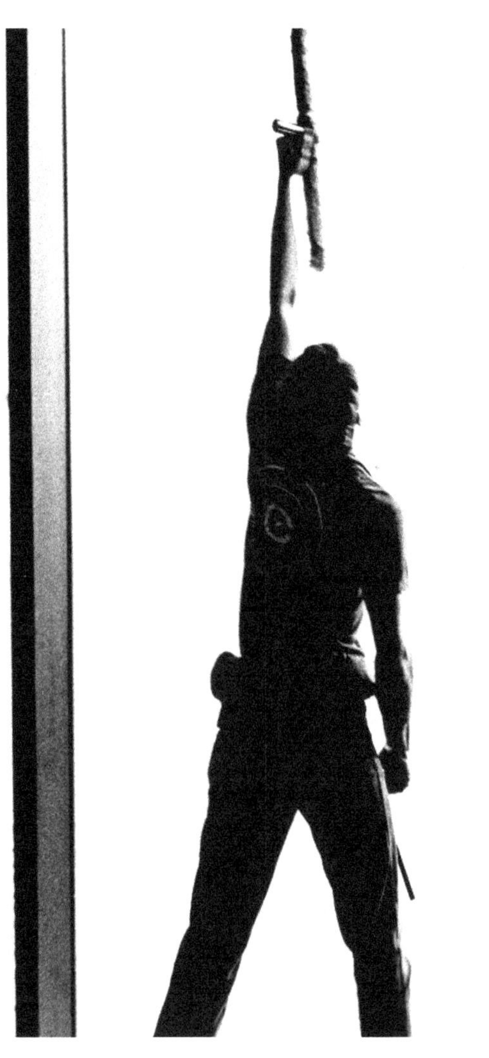

Window Cleaner
Atlanta

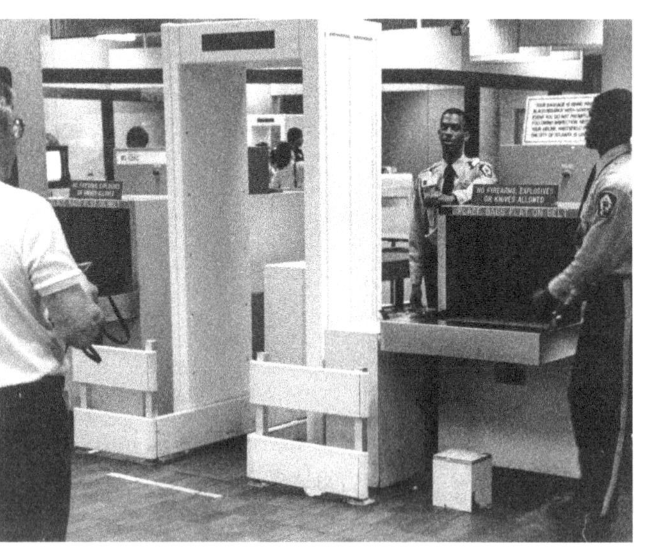

Pre 9/11 Security
Atlanta

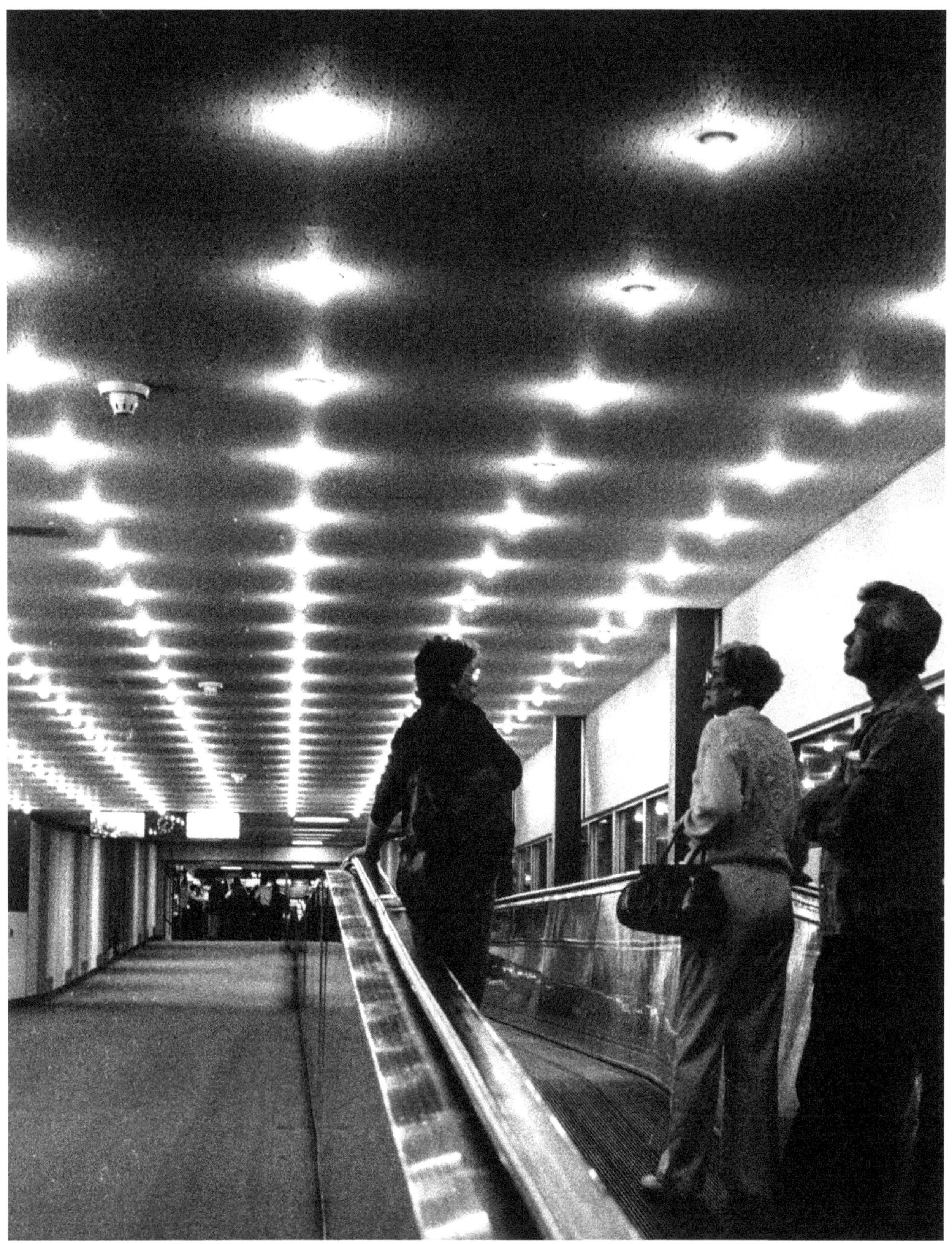

People Mover
Dallas Love Field

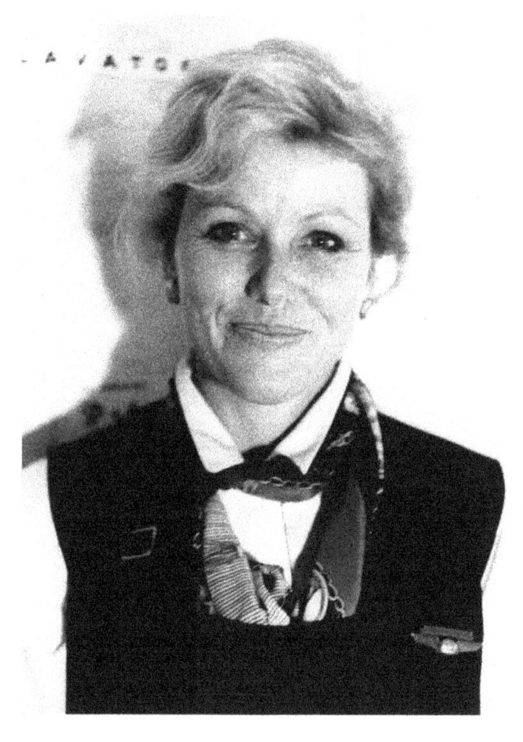

Washington Nat to Atlanta. She had been flying for 12 years. She had a daughter (19) and a son (9). Felt 13 and 14 were the most difficult years.

Shine man O'Hare. Business was slow today, but "you gotta do sumpin". He had lived in Chicago for 35 years, never been anywhere else. "Do they have busses in Atlanta?"

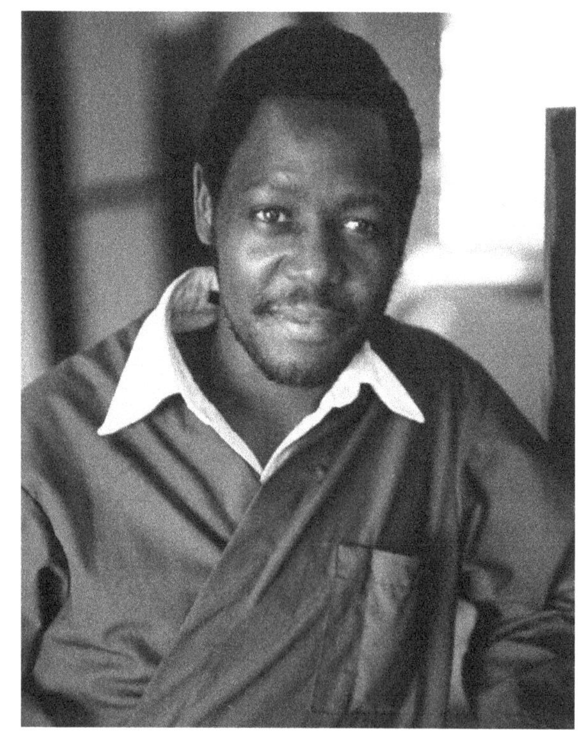

Shine Lady in Dallas Ft. Worth.
Management Student
at North Texas State.

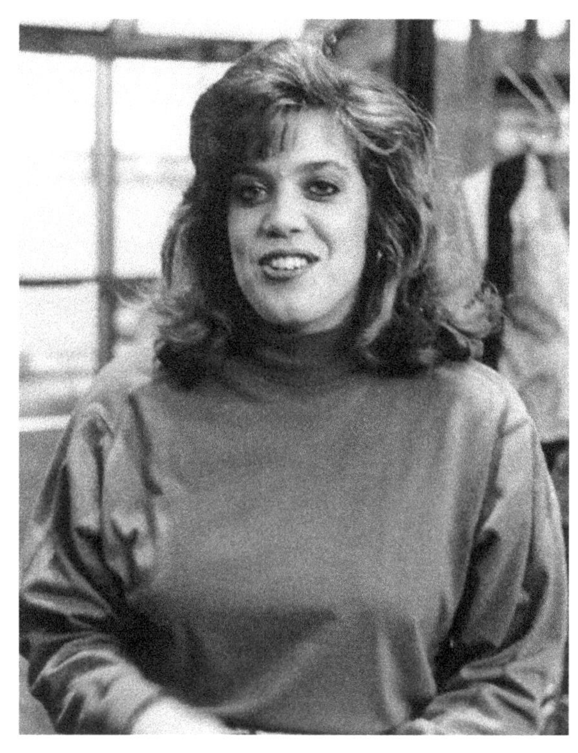

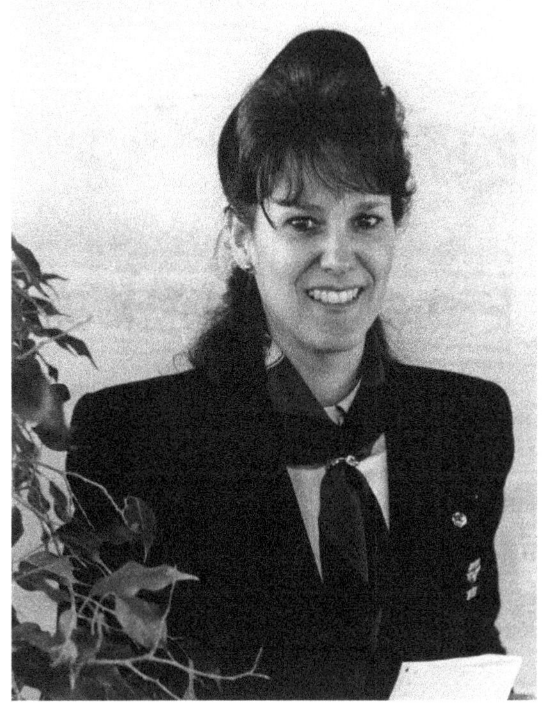

She had been flying for 17 years and was worried about the financial stability of Eastern Airlines. "I just try to do my job the best I can every day." Samual Gompers, a founder of the American labor movement, was once quoted as saying "The cruelest condition management can impose on labor, is failure to make a profit."

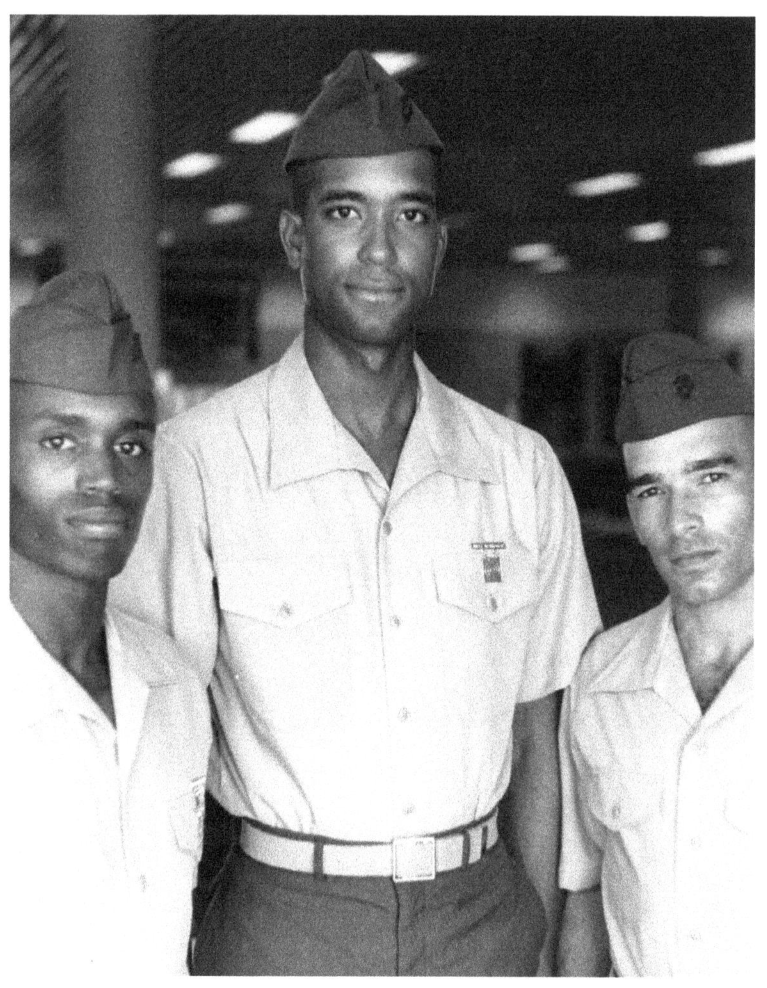

One was from Cleveland, one from
Cincinnati, and one from Puerto Rico.
They had just graduated from Marine
boot camp that morning. When I asked
them if I could take their picture, they all
stood at attention.

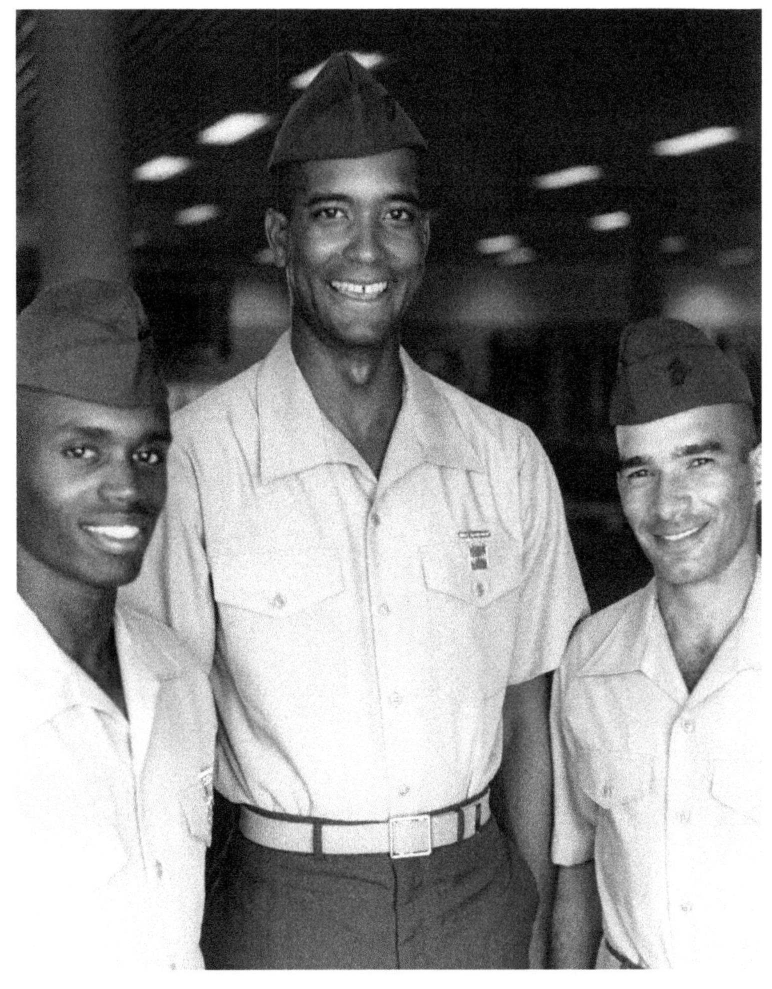

After I took the first shot, I said, "Come on
guys, boot camp is over." They all laughed for
this second shot.

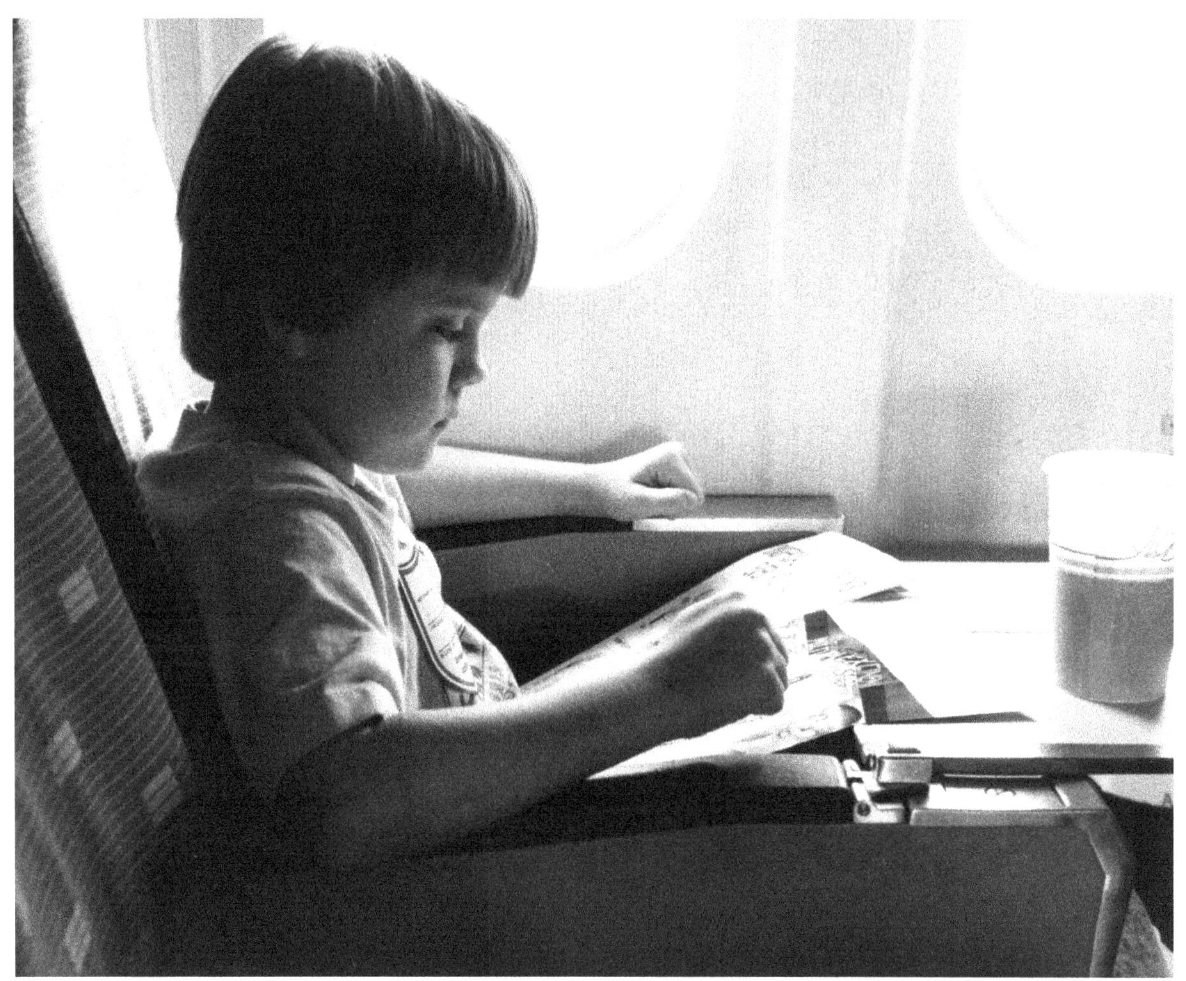

He was traveling to see his grandmother. He was a little
scared. We talked about baseball cards, and when we got
off the plane, he told me I was a nice guy.
Atlanta to Dallas

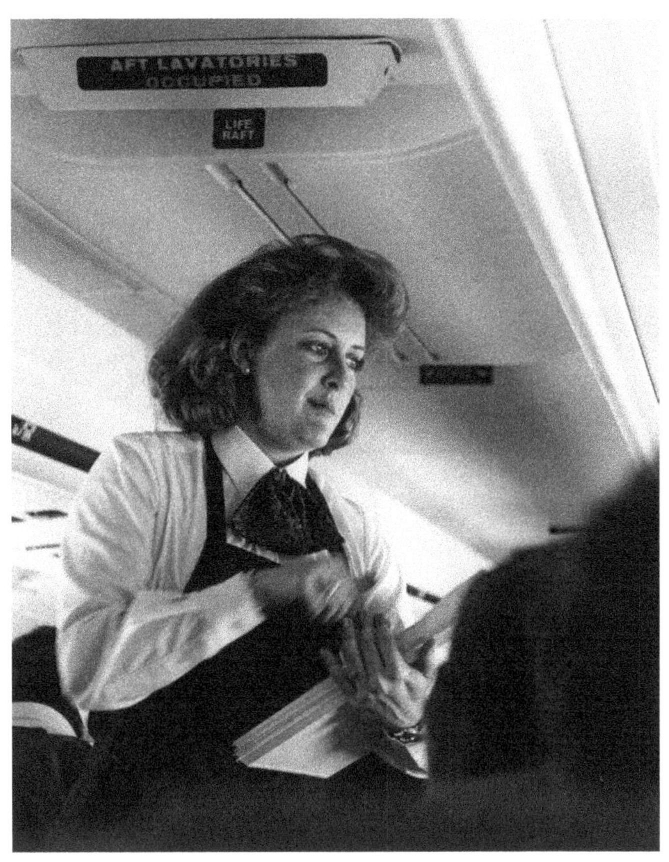

Snacks
Lexington to Atlanta

She is explaining to the
first-class passenger why he
did not get a first class meal.

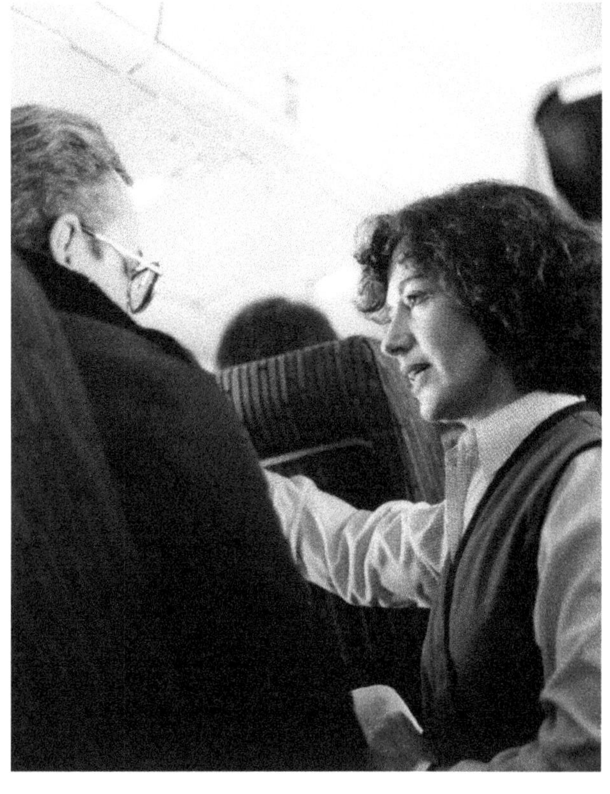

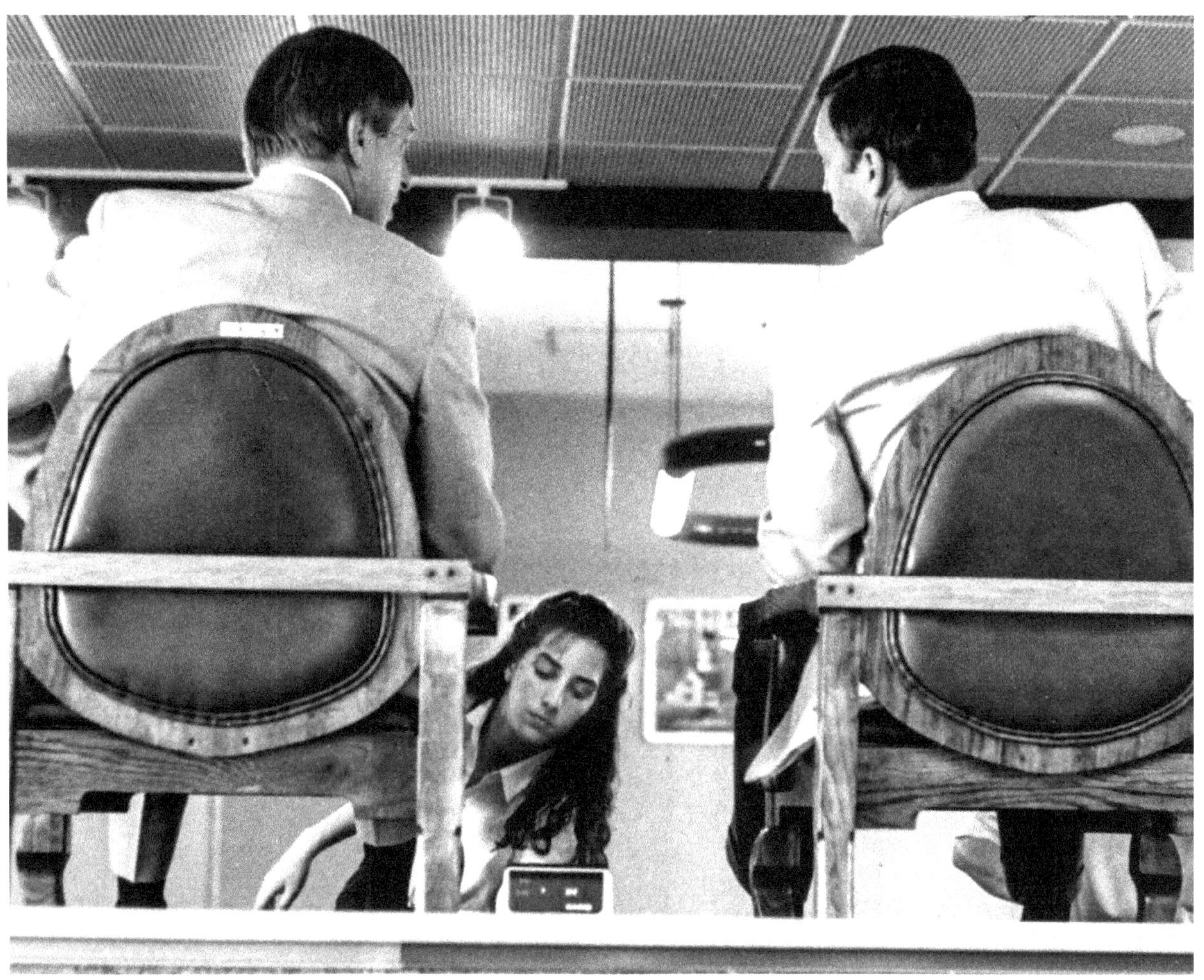

Shoe Shine Person
Dallas

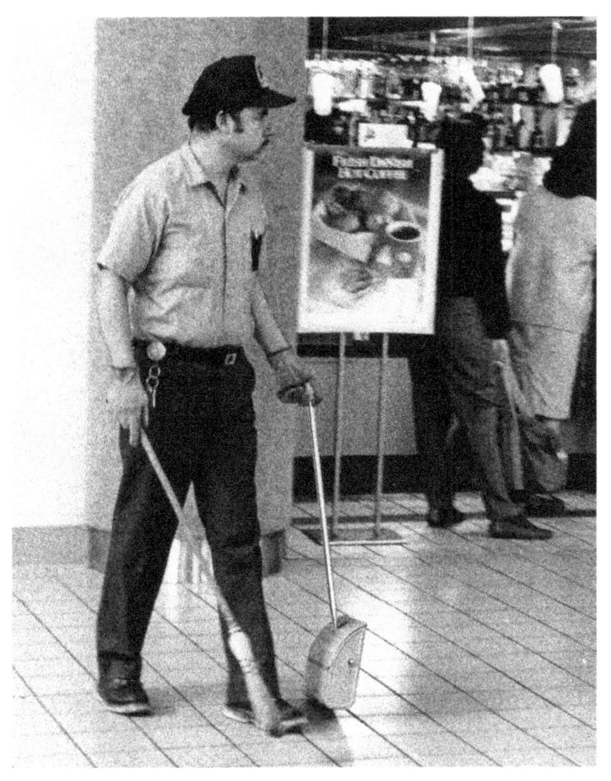

Clean up in Los Angeles

Men like this were invisible to the travelers, but without them, the system would not have worked.

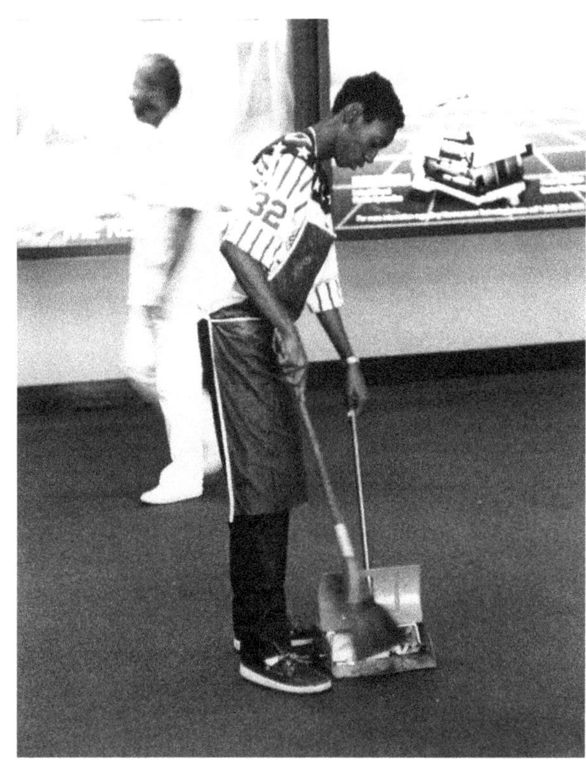

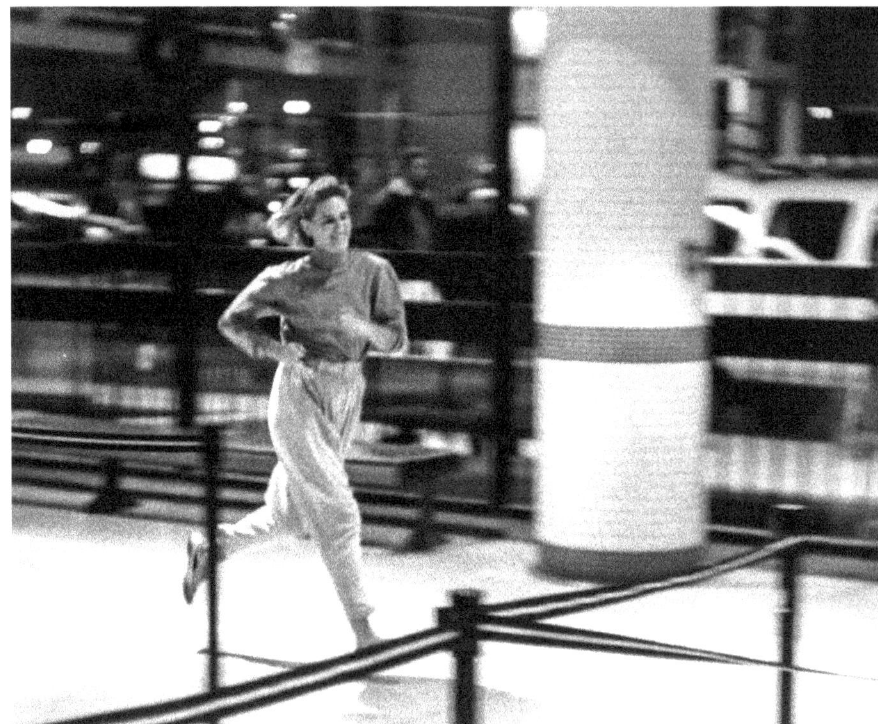

Runner in
Los Angeles

Small Traveler,
Big Bird

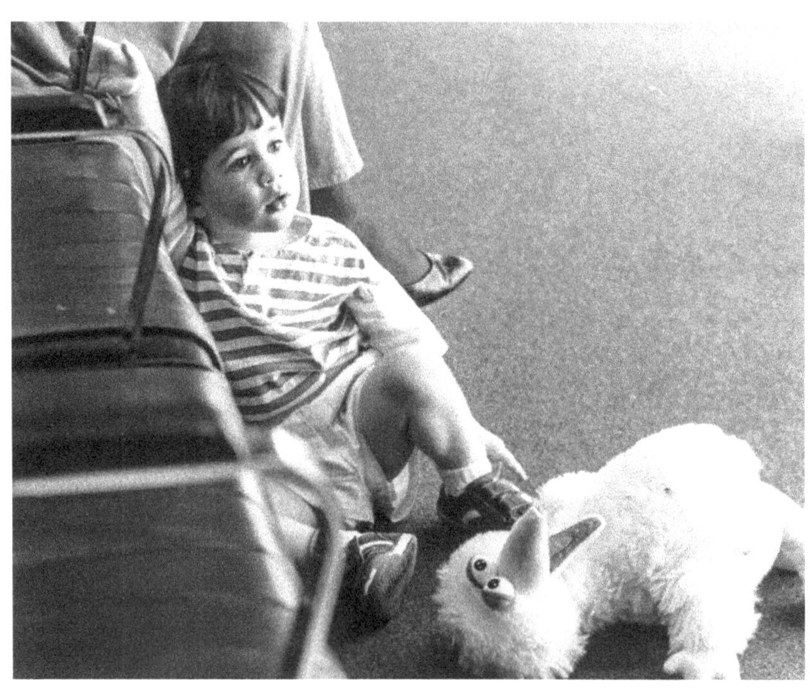

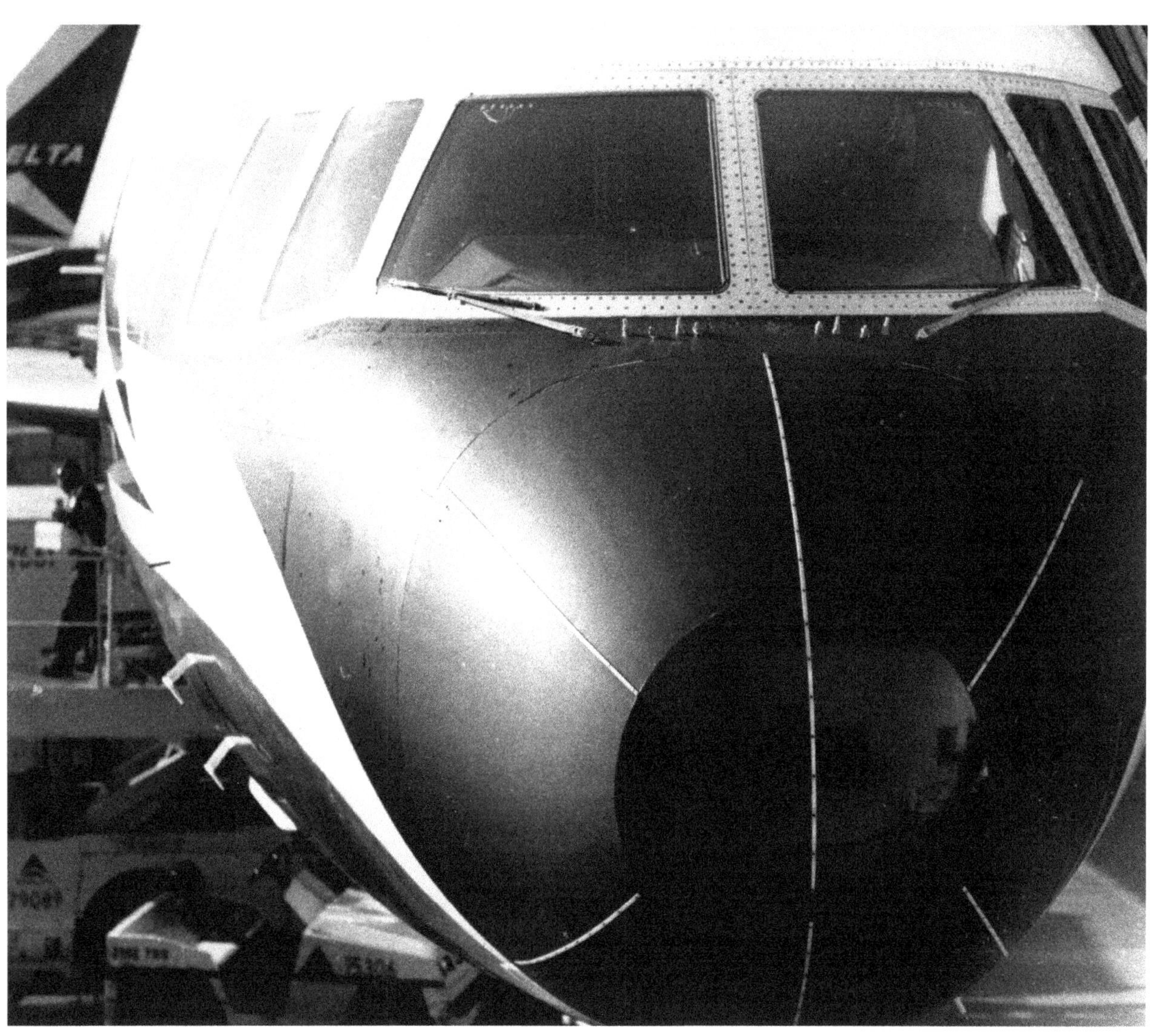

Big Bird
Los Angeles

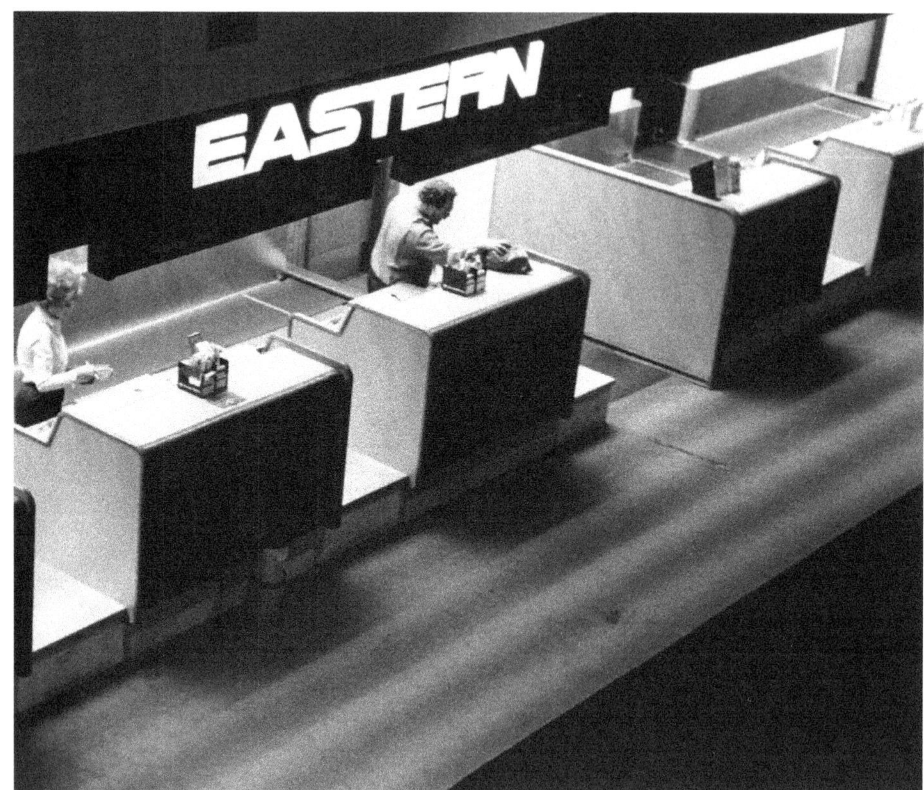

Eastern Ticket Counter, Dead Man Walking
Huntsville, AL

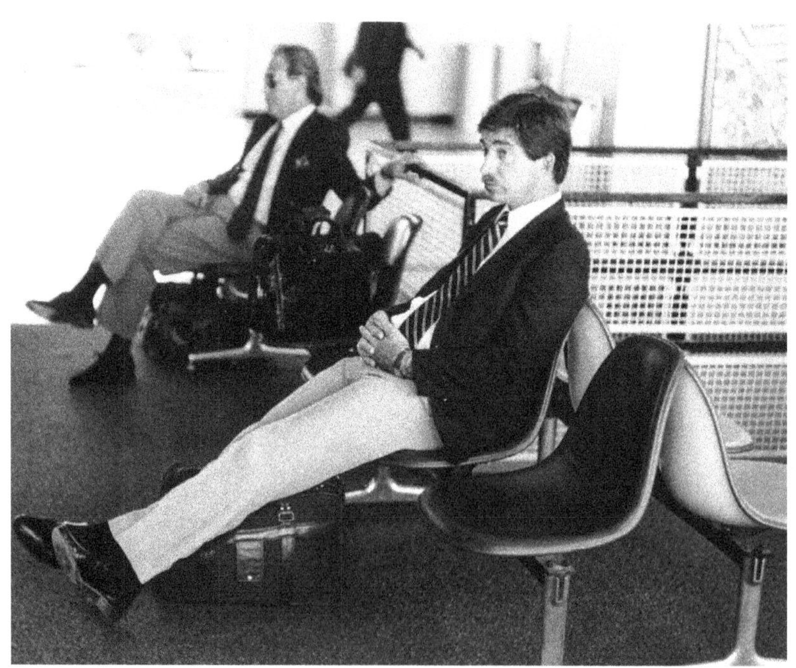

Stand By
O'Hare

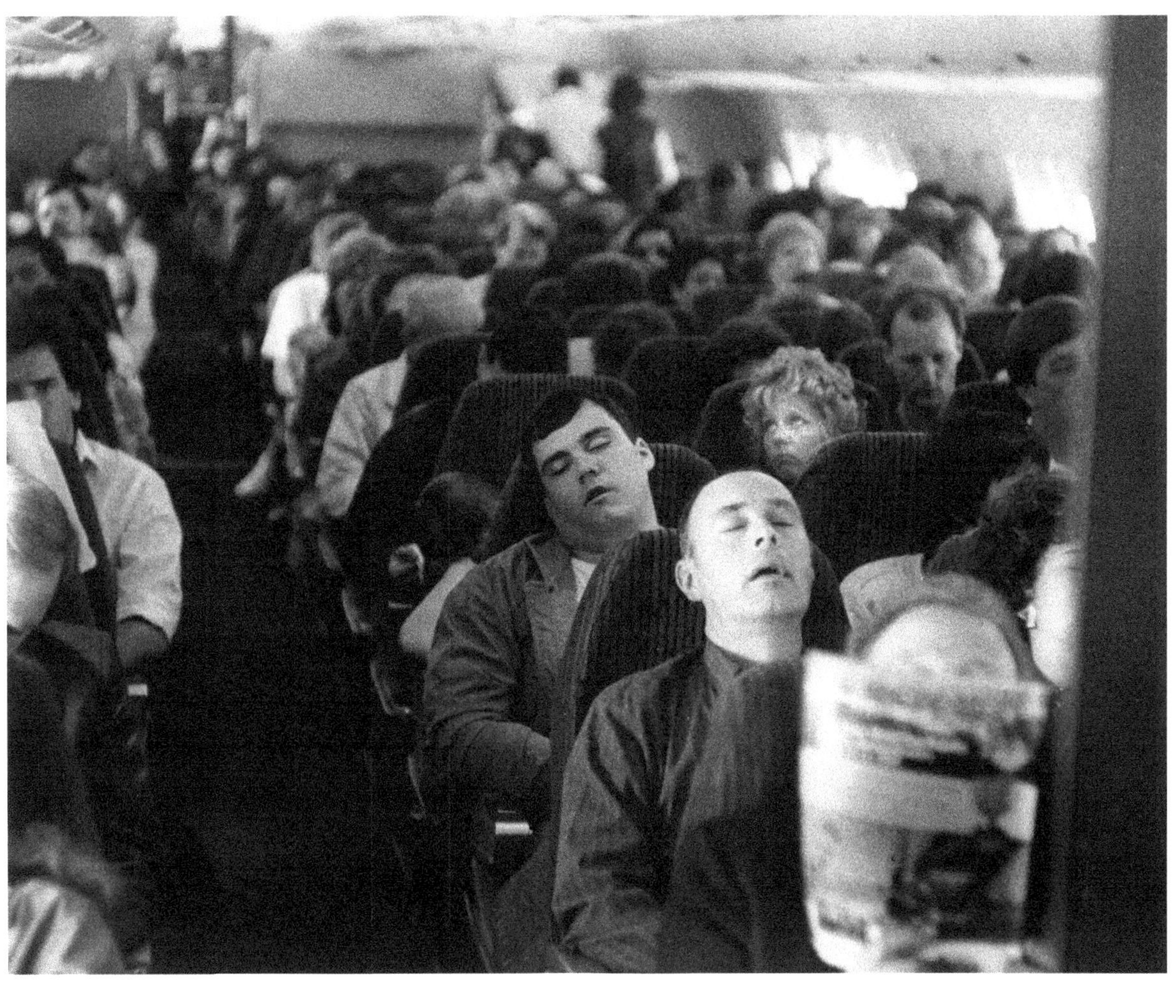

Long Flight from Los Angeles to Atlanta

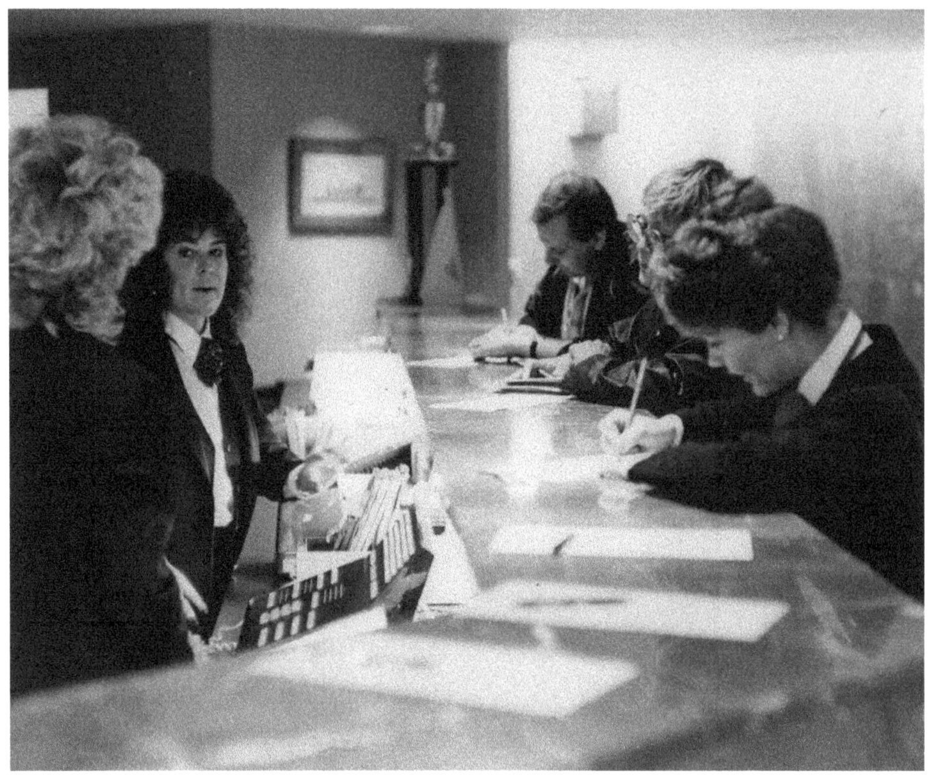

Flight Crew check in, hotel, Huntsville
By the '80s the life of the crew was long days with
endless check ins.

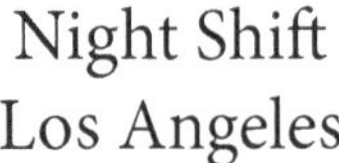

Night Shift
Los Angeles

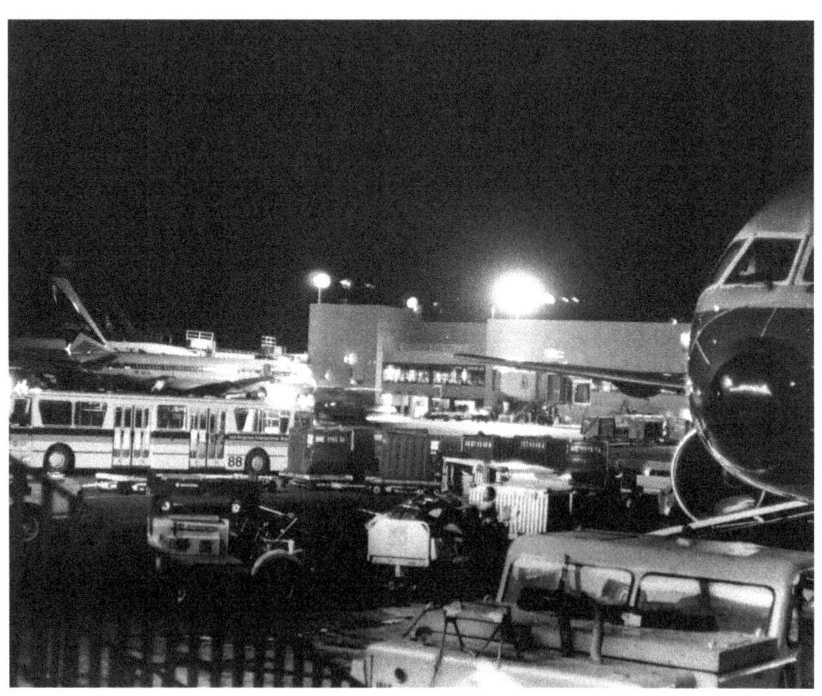

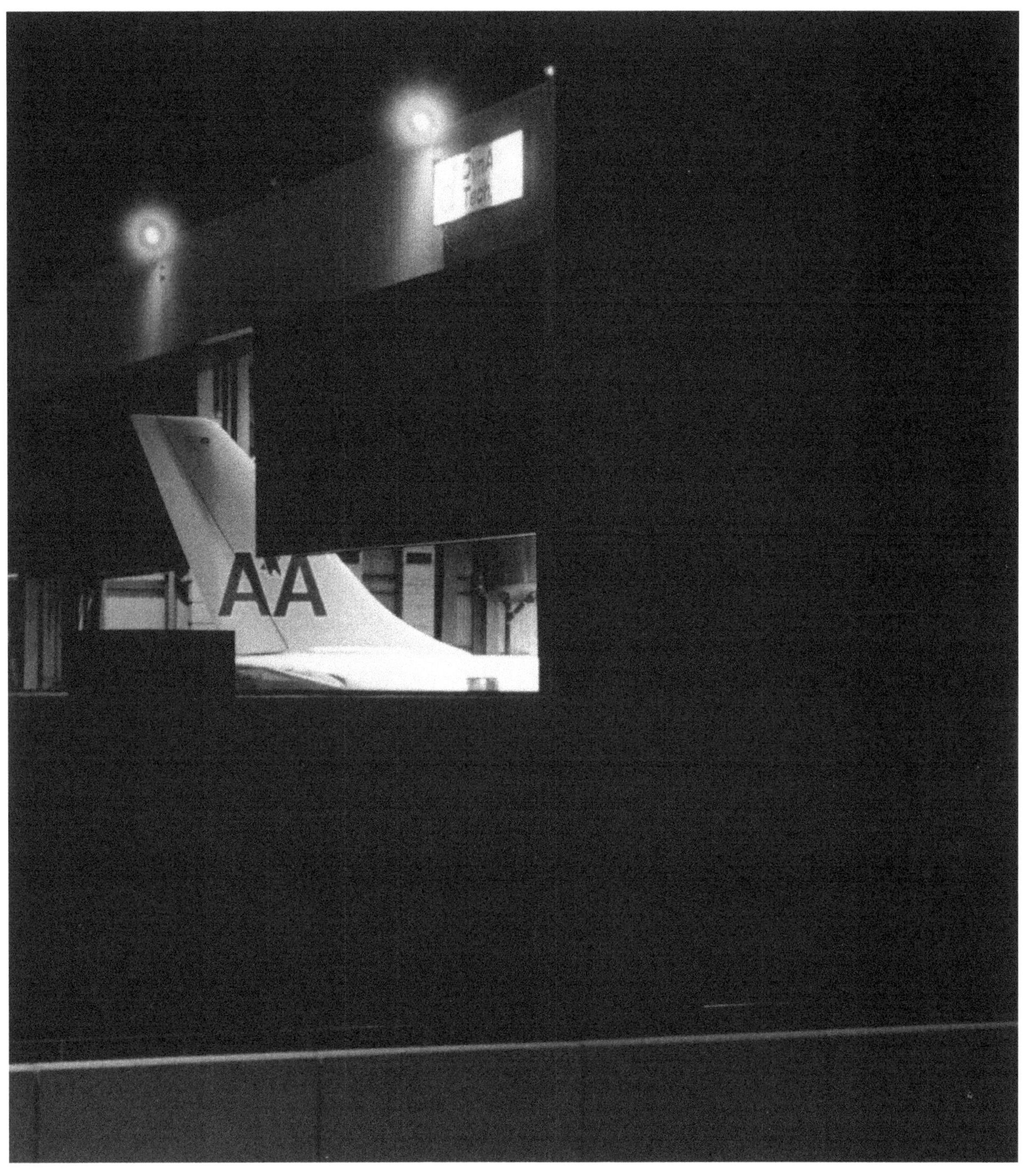

American Airlines Plane Tail

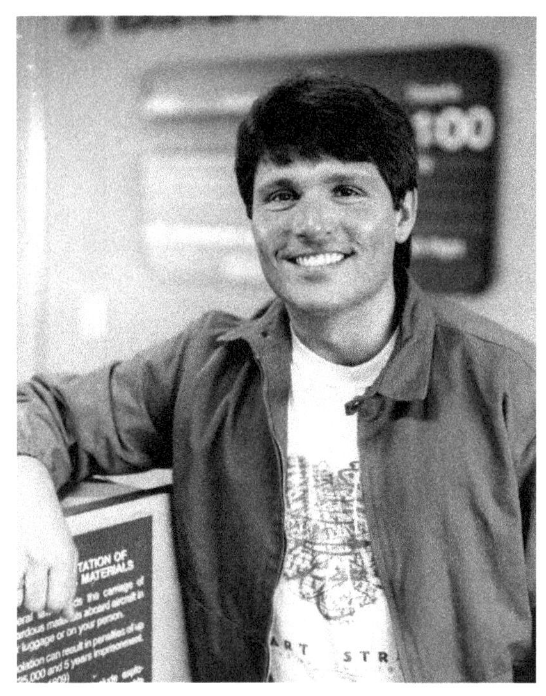

He was the son of a missionary and attended Wheaton Bible College. He had been a missionary himself (France) and was now with a software company. He trained doctors on how the use their software.

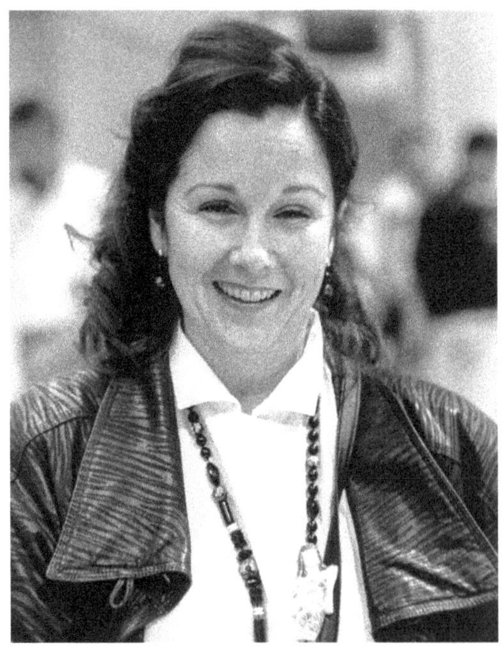

She had been a business consultant in the medical field for 18 years. She entered the field after she was turned down for medical school. She told me that she traveled a lot, frequently worked for eighteen hours per day when she was on the road. She shared that her business life left little time for personal life and **no** time to have a family.

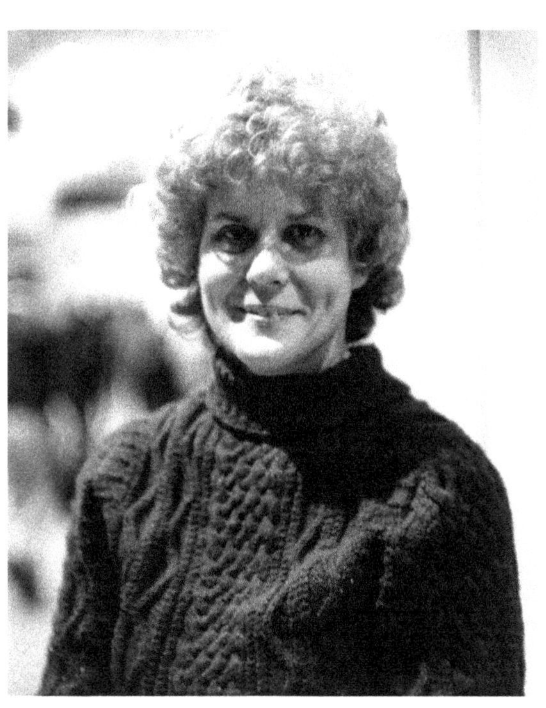

She was flying to California for Christmas with her family. She and her husband were separated, and she still loved him. He had a substance abuse problem, and she was not going to go back with him until he dealt with it.

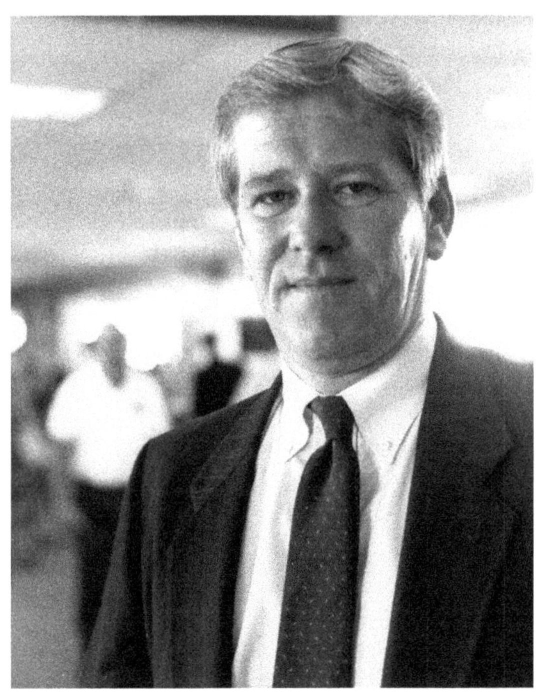

He was a computer sales executive who had transferred to California from the Midwest. His family was "adjusting."

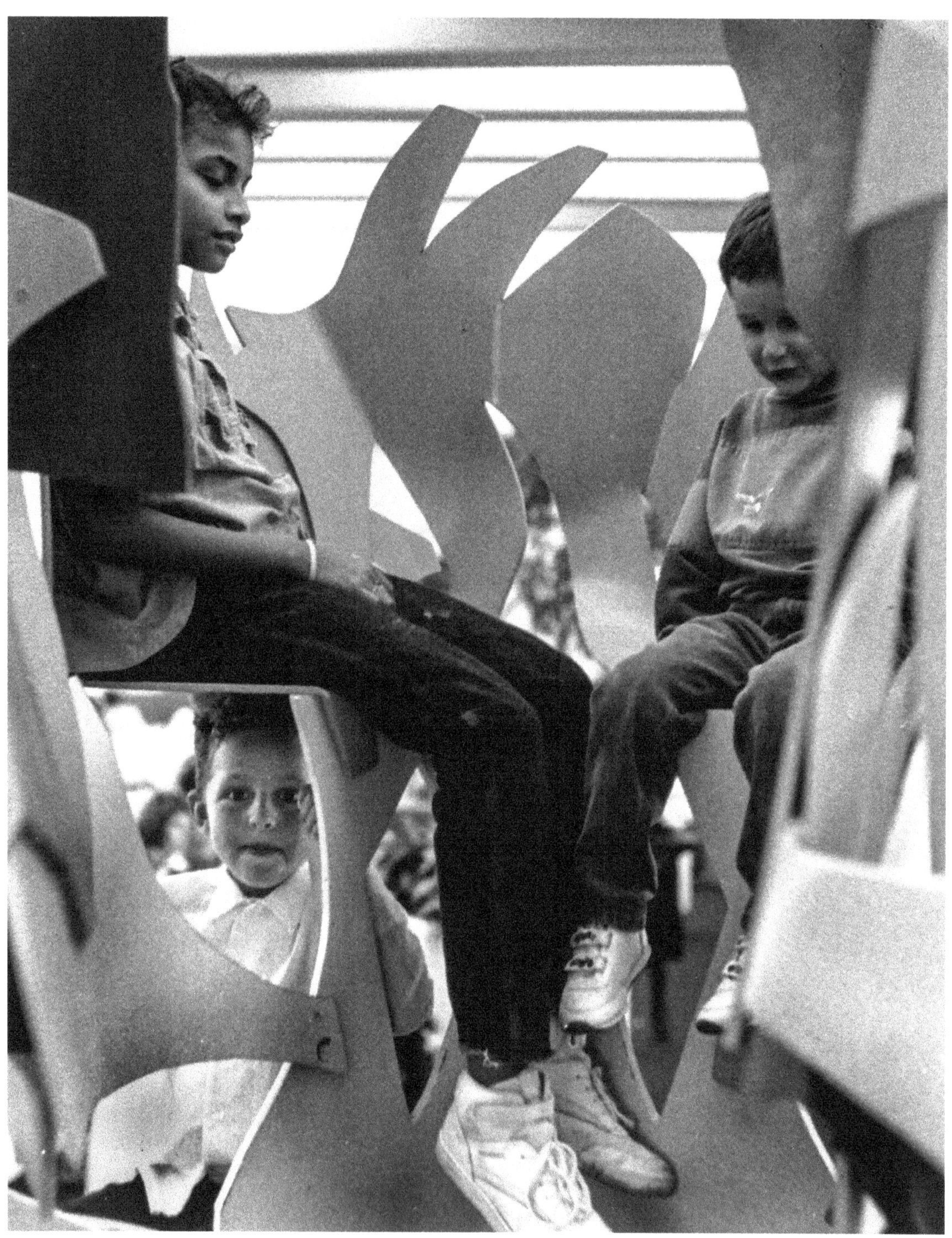

Sculpture, Kids Playing
Miami

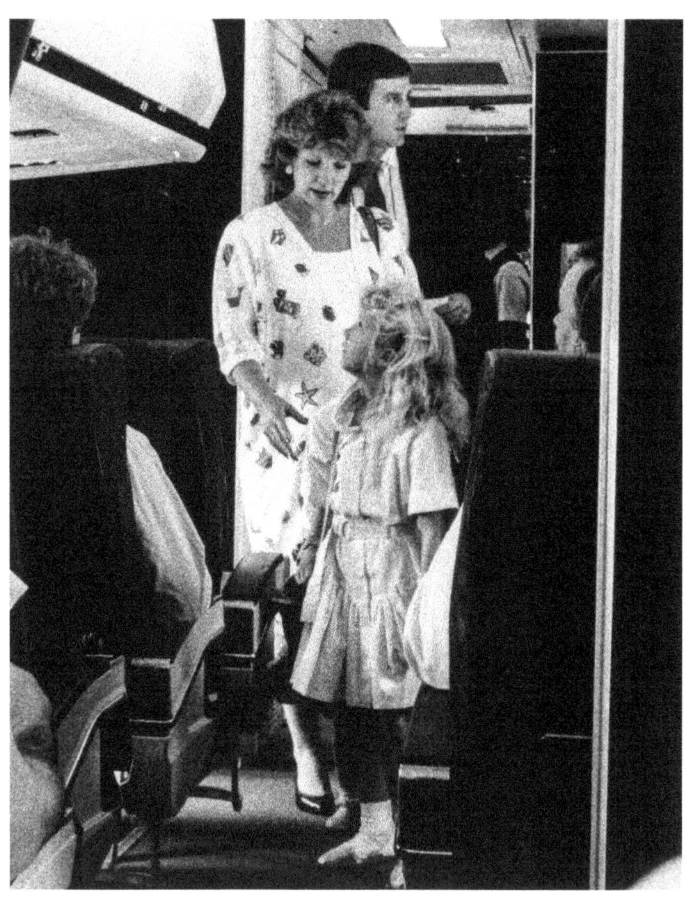

Family boarding
Atlanta to Houston

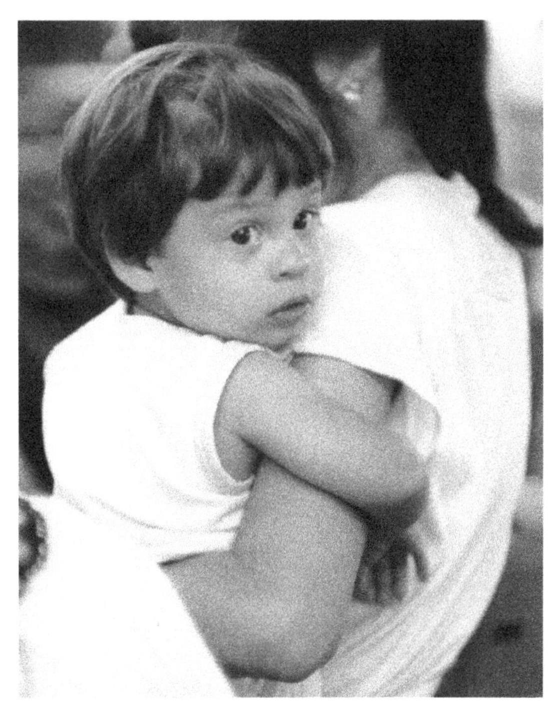

Carry on San Juan, Puerto
Rico "All carry on must be
able to fit in the overhead
compartment or under the
seat in front of you."

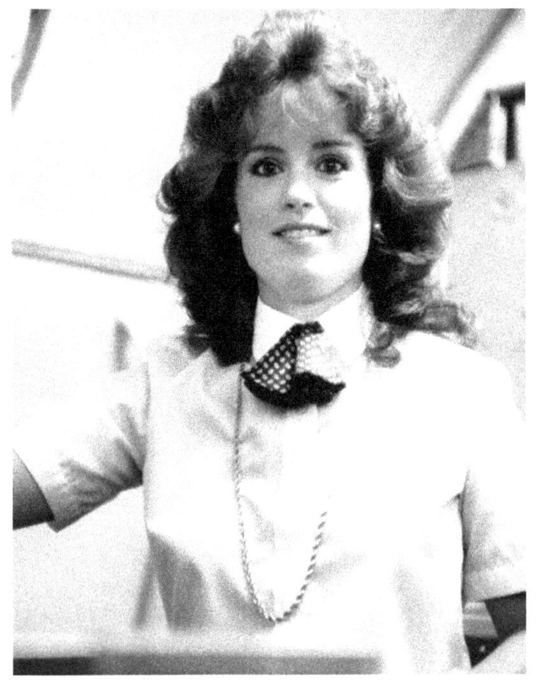

She was just starting a 6 day trip. Based in Atlanta, she had a 15 month old son, who missed her when she was gone. She left before he woke up for her trips, to avoid tears (hers and his).

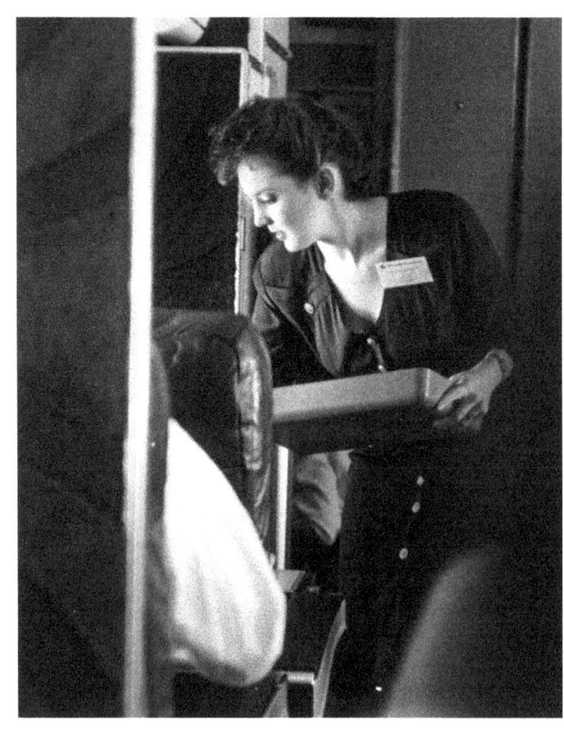

New flight attendant
Houston to Atlanta

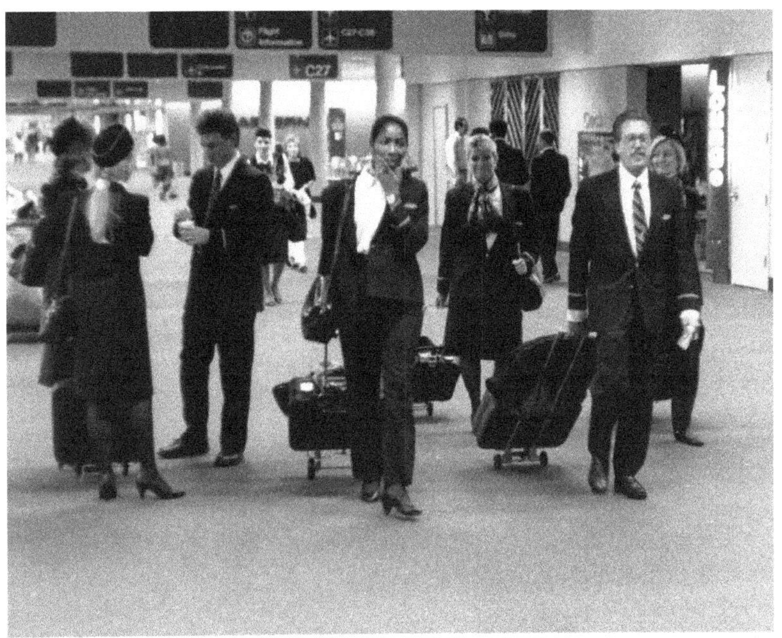

Eastern FAs going to work. In the early years, it was considered a *glamorous* job. The pay was relatively high (for a young female, which was the only people they hired at the time) and they got to travel. They were hired for their looks and their personality.

Flight deck service Although it was nowhere near as common as assumed, there was always an assumption that there were affairs between the pilots (almost all male in the early days) and flight attendants. The old joke was a pilot, thinking he was on a private communication, said "Beautiful, bring me some of your hot coffee and your hot love," which was heard by the entire plane. As the flight attendant rushed to the flight deck to inform him that is was being broadcast, someone shouted, "Hey Beautiful, you forgot the coffee."
Atlanta to St. Louis

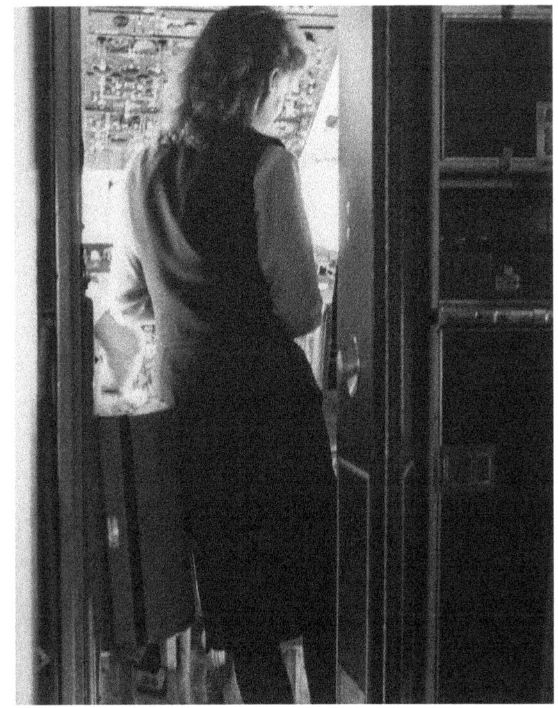

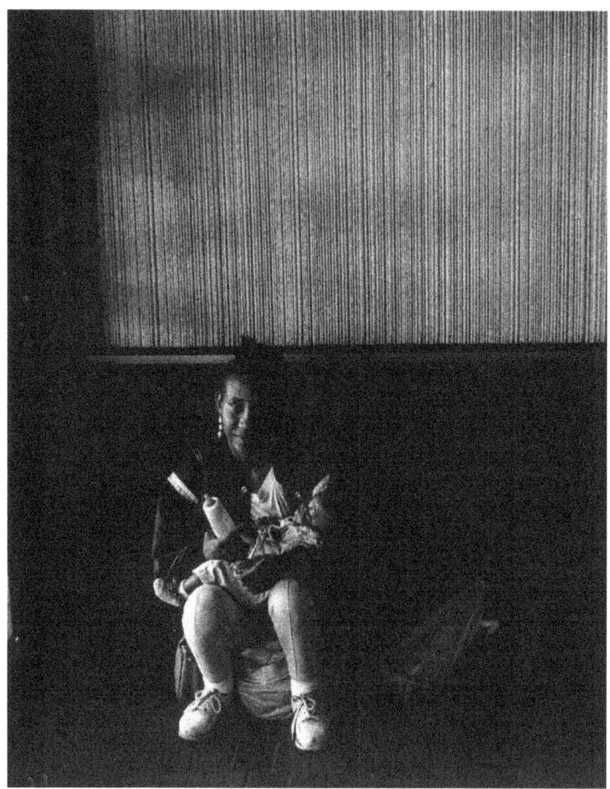

Small mother, big airport
Atlanta Airport

Washington National

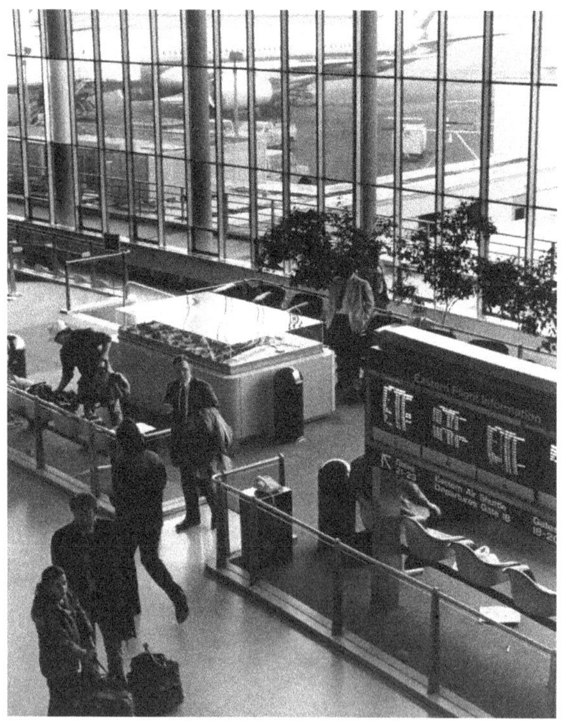

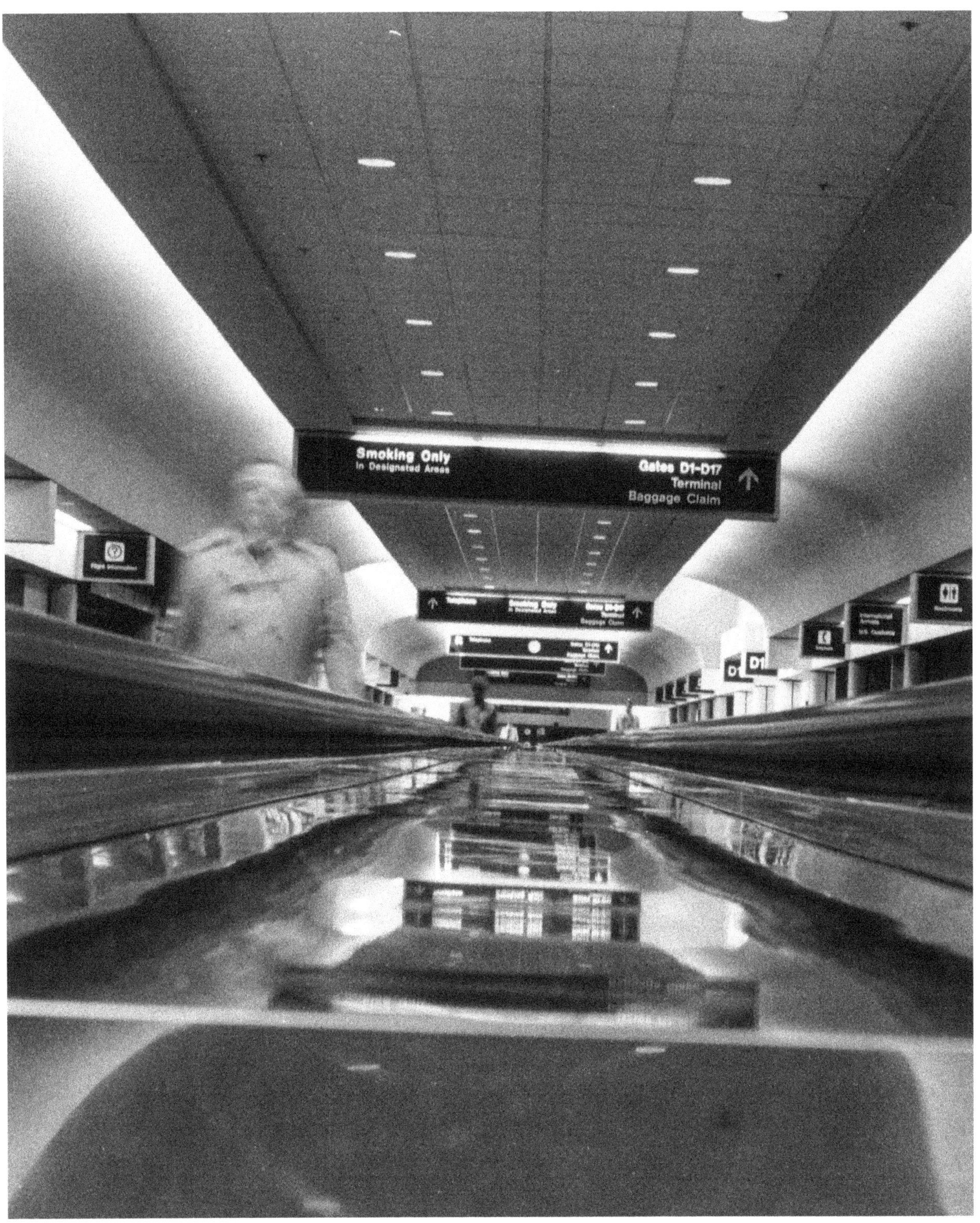

People Mover
Cincinnati

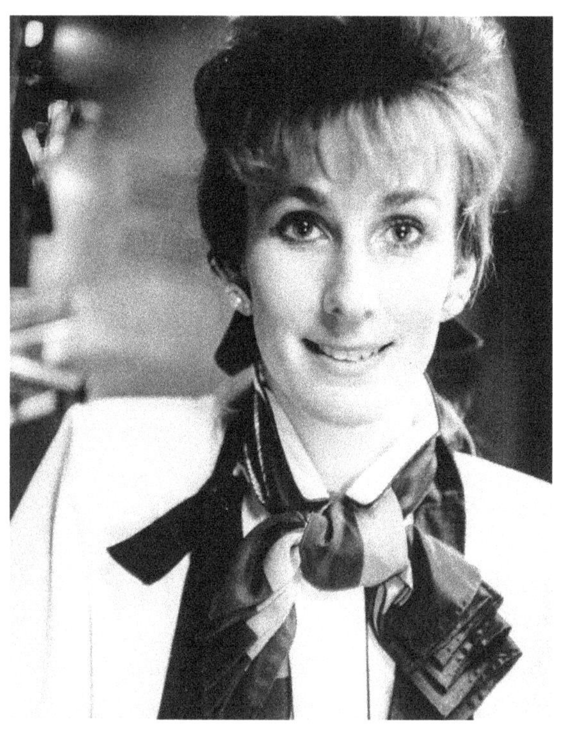

She was from Yorkshire, England, and had married a U. S. Marine Sergeant. She moved to Atlanta in September of 1989 and was very homesick, but couldn't go home until September of 1990.

Atlanta Ionosphere Club
"I take such a bad picture."

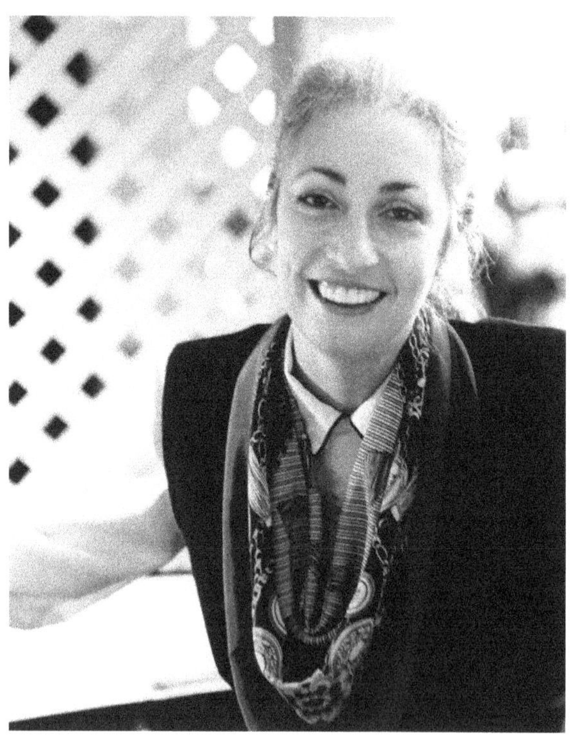

Los Angeles to Atlanta
She had been a recovery room
nurse since the divorce (5 years
ago) and was worried about the
health care problems facing the
country.

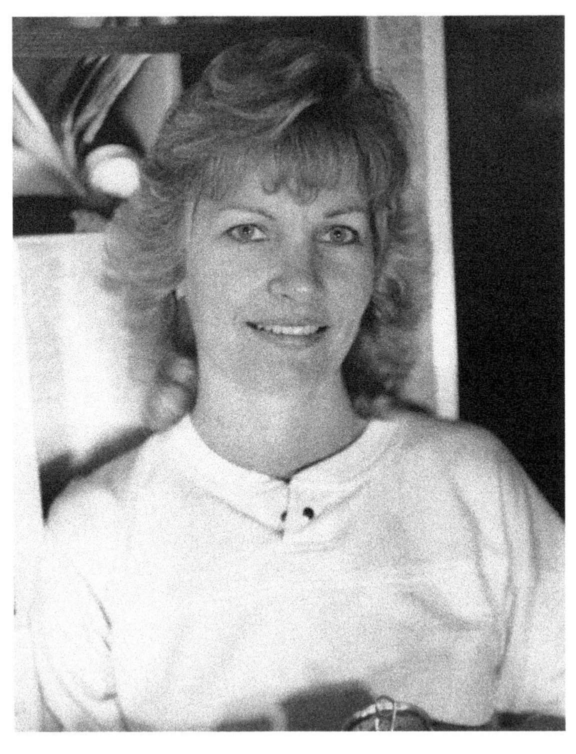

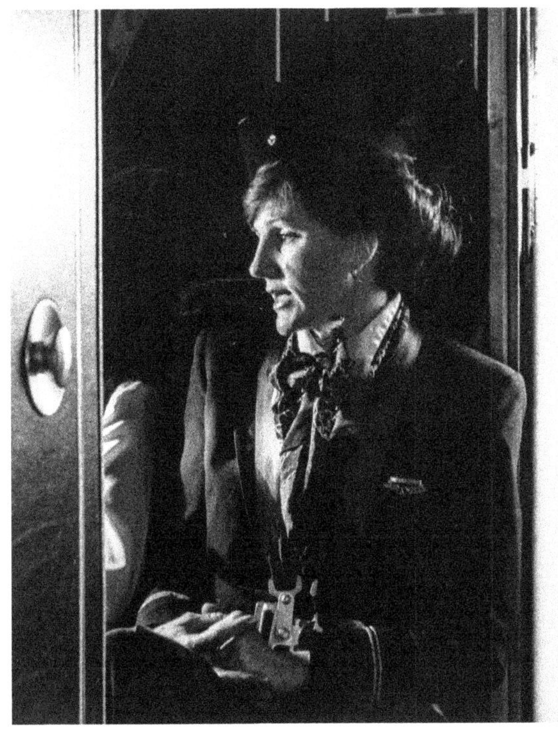

As the industry matured, their
pay was reduced to the point
where there was a two tiered
system in most airlines, with
some of the younger hires paid
as though it was a "part time"
job, since they did not work a
standard 40 hour week.

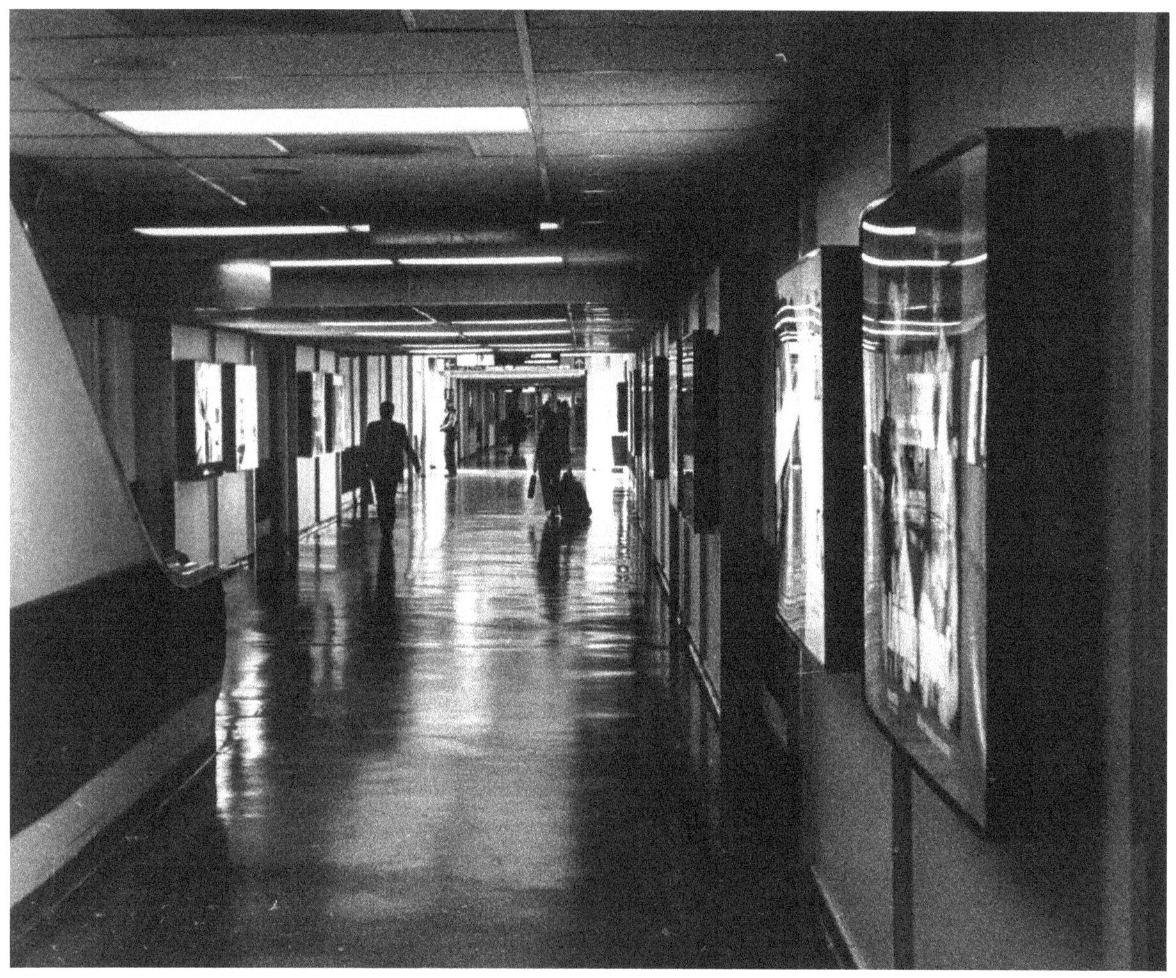

Corridor
Washington National

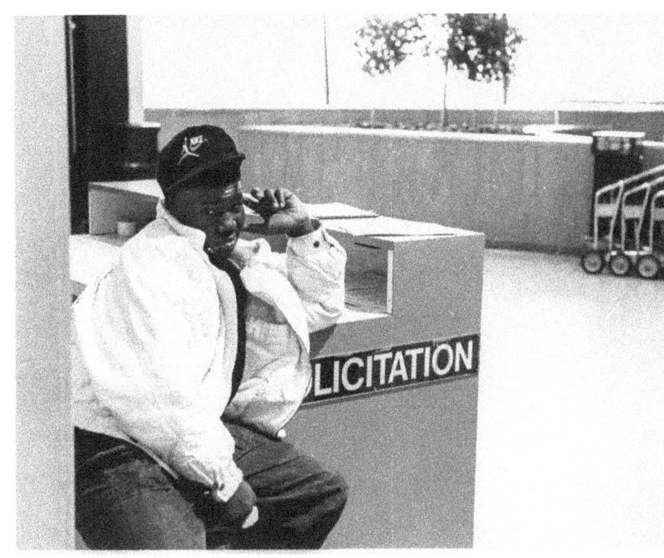

No solicitation, just waiting on an
arriving passenger

Good Night
Miami

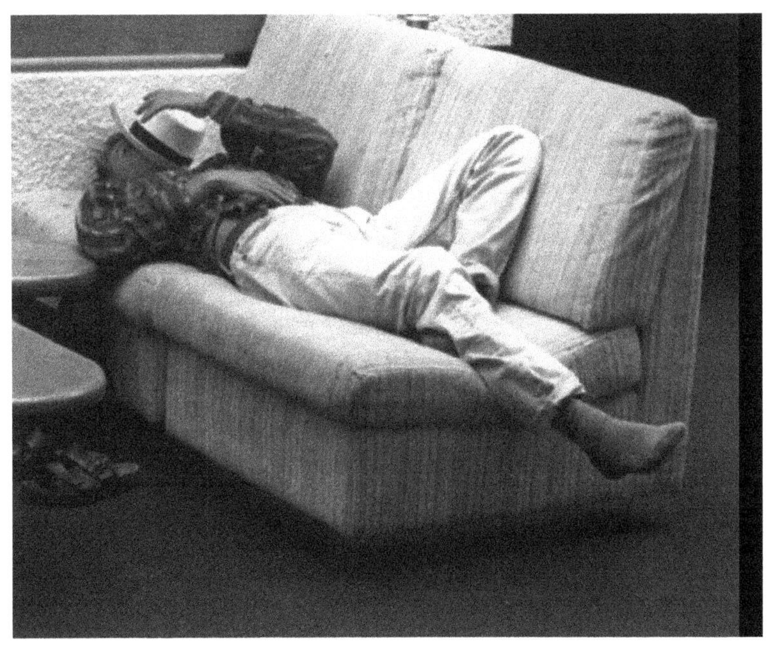

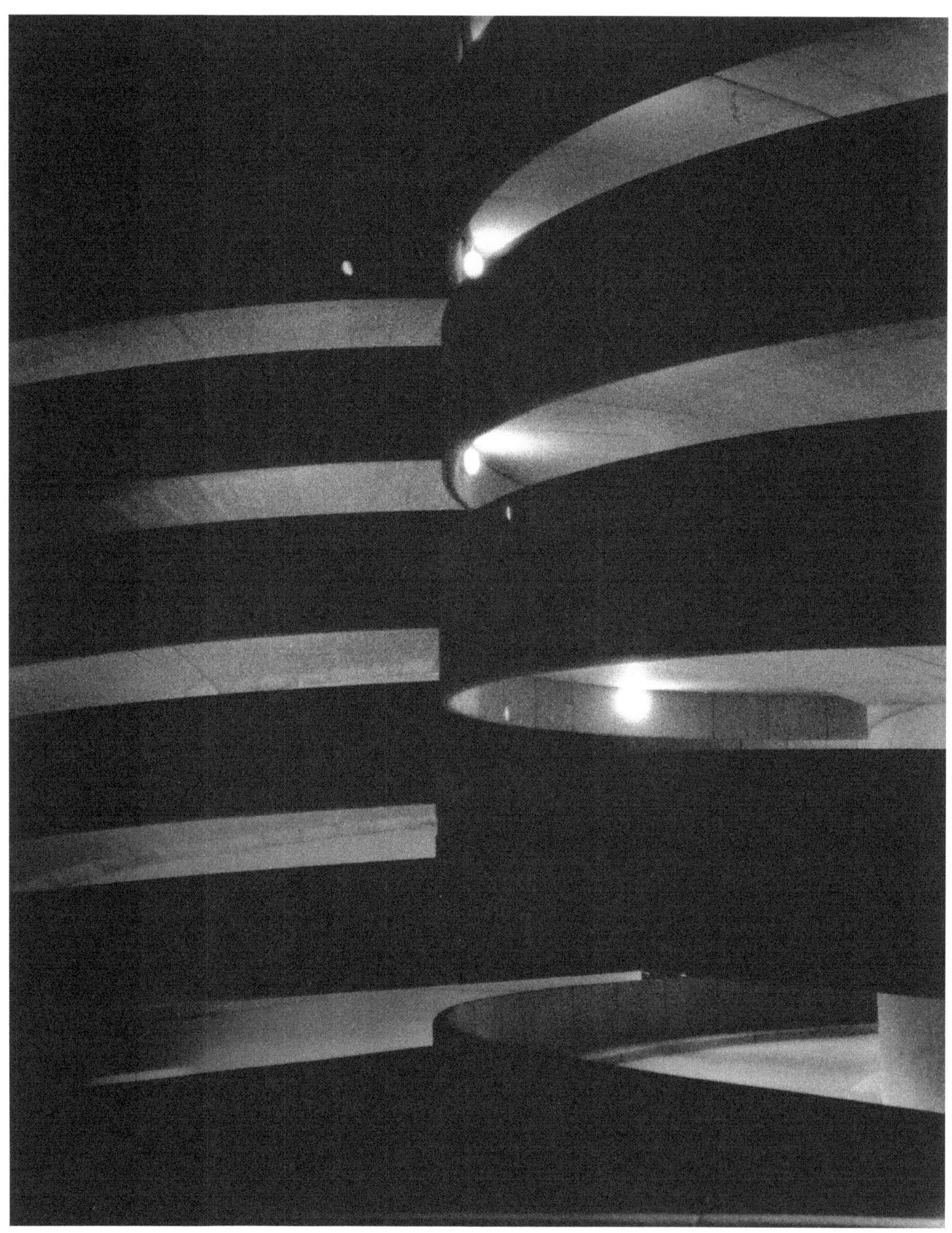

Parking
Phoenix

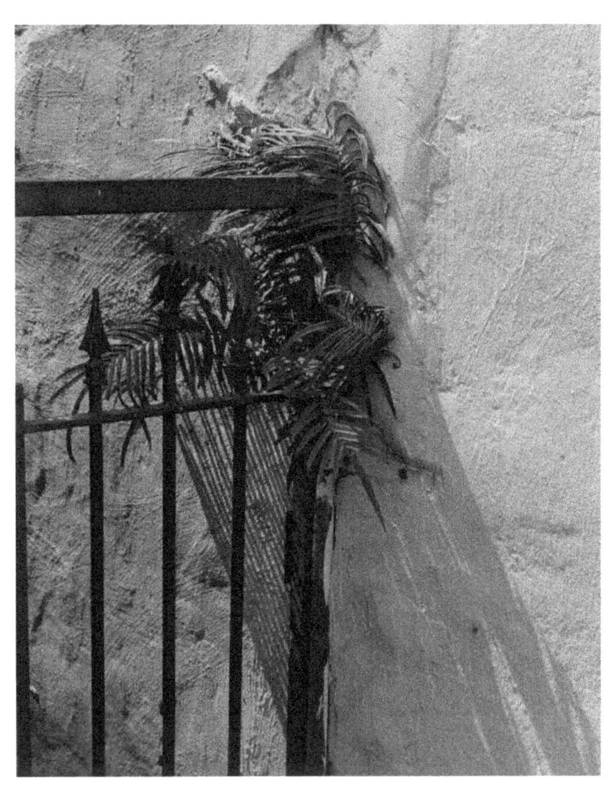

Iron Work
French Quarter

Superdome Convention
New Orleans

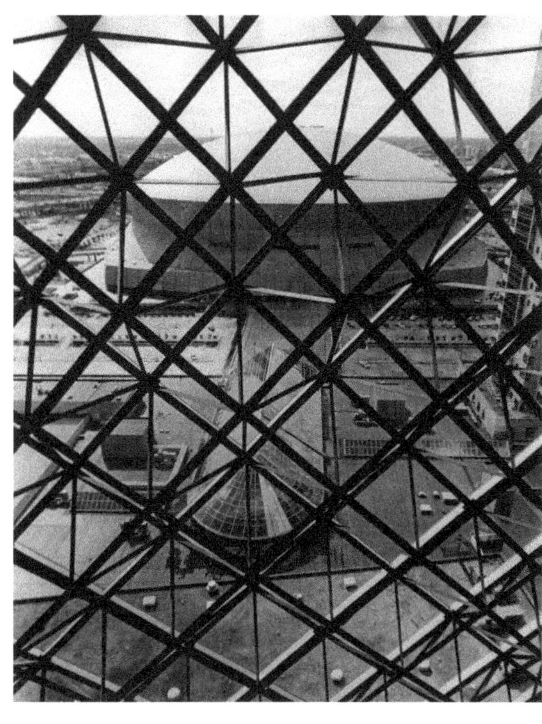

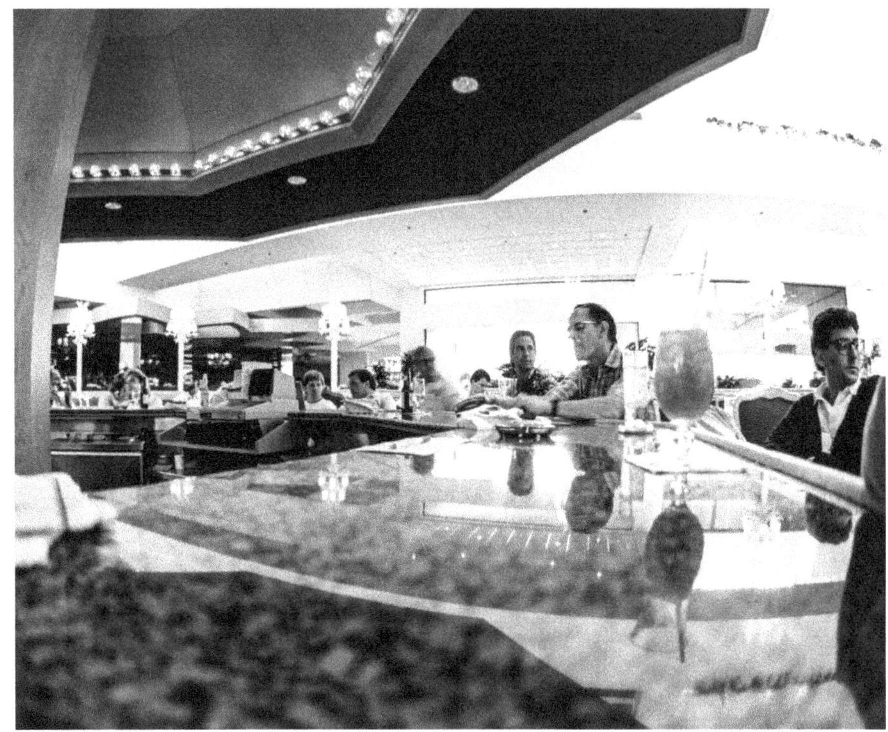

So this guy came into the bar and said to the
bartender, "What's the strongest thing you
got back there?" Without batting an eye, the
bartender said, "I don't know, try the coffee."
Bar, Red Lion Inn, Costa Mesa, CA

O'Hare Business conference

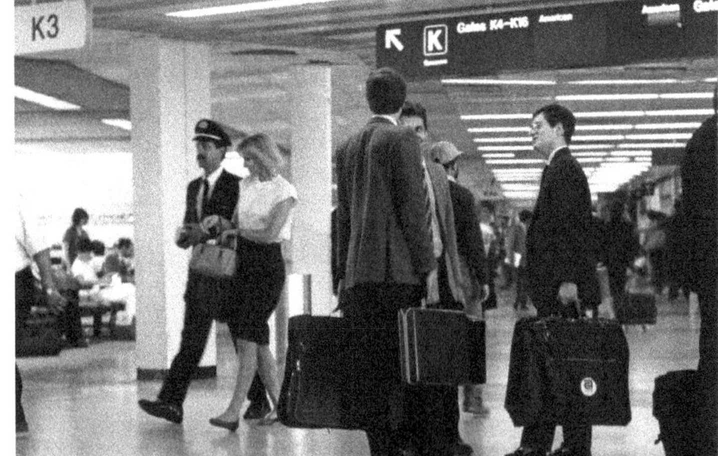

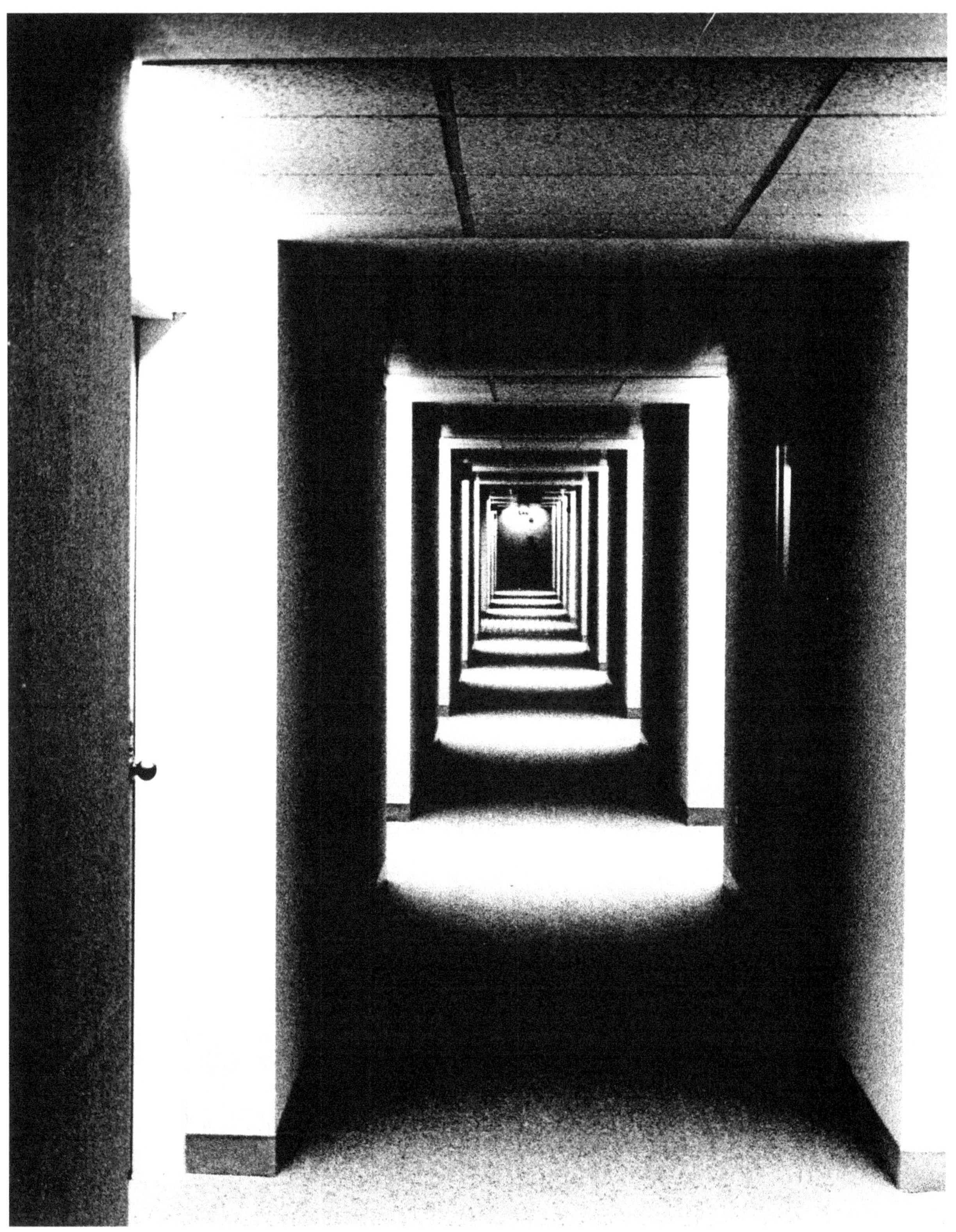

Hampton Inn
Schaumburg, Il

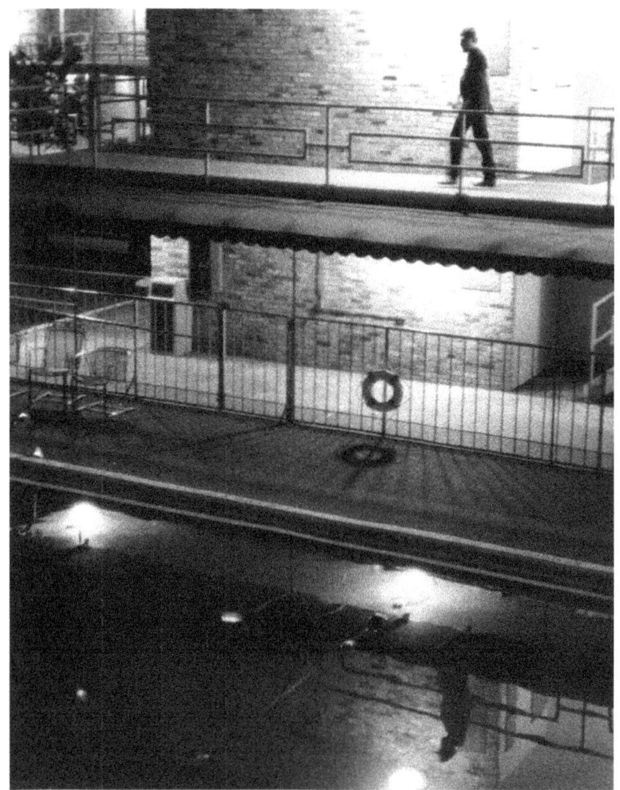

Pool, Holiday Inn
Paducah, KY.

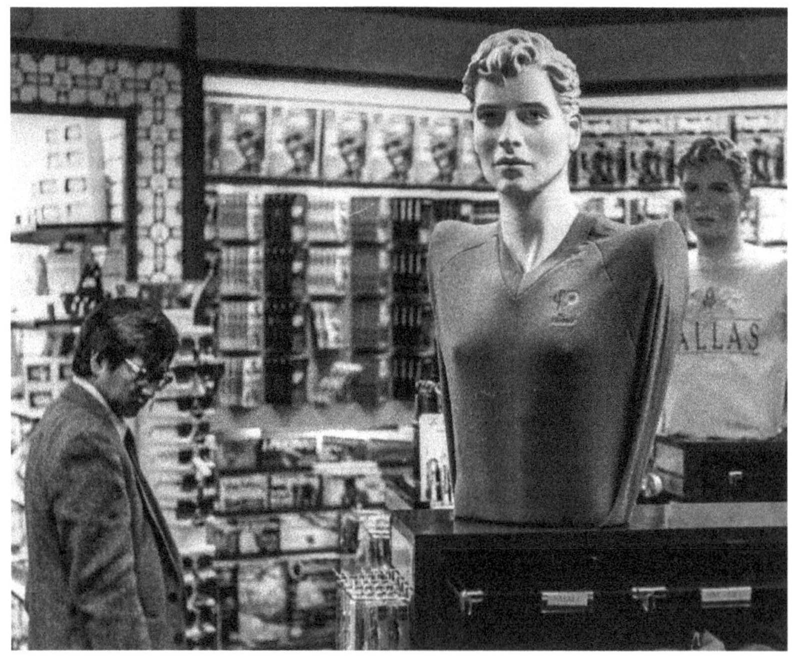

Mannequins in the Gift Shop
DFW Gift Shop

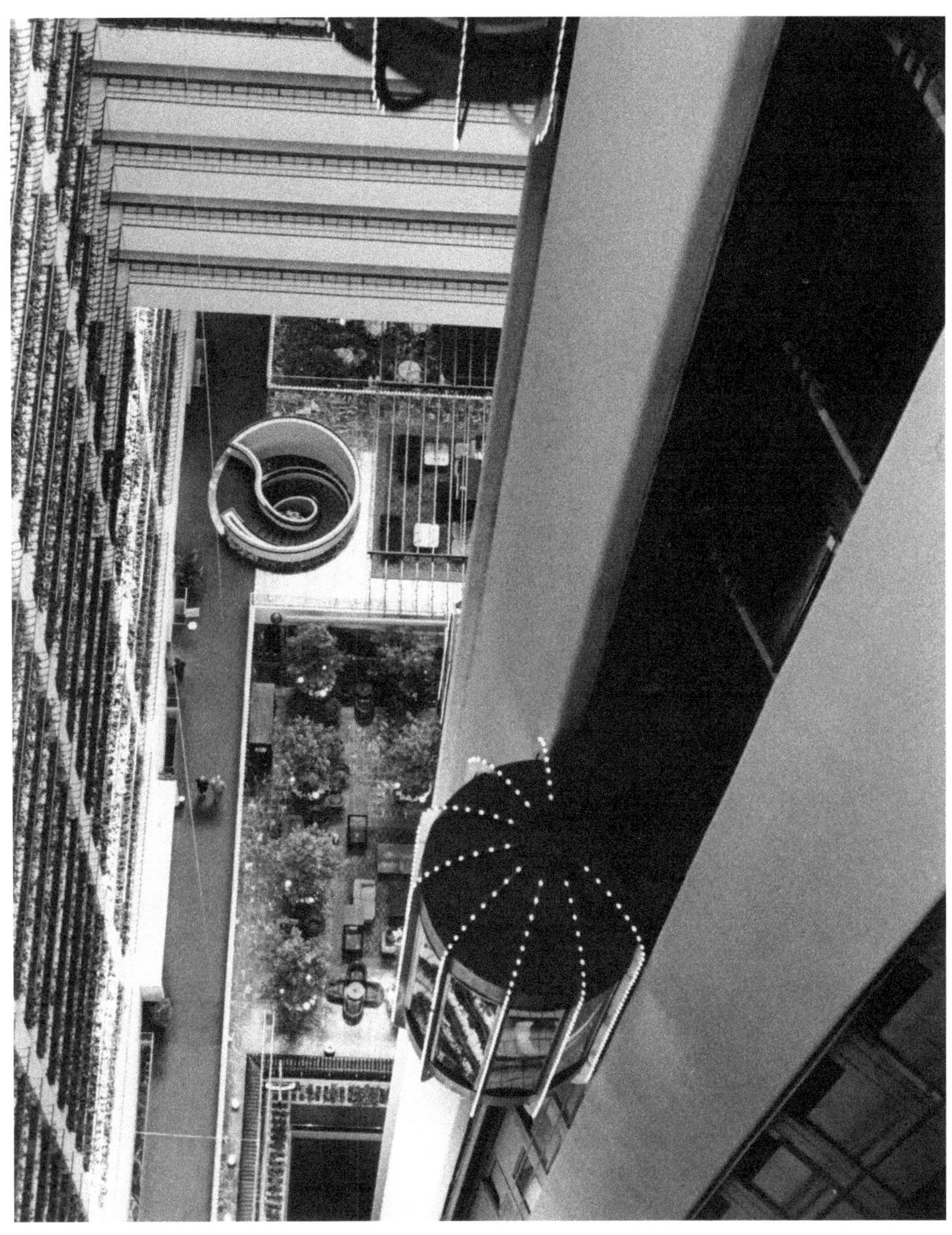

Marriott Marquis
New York

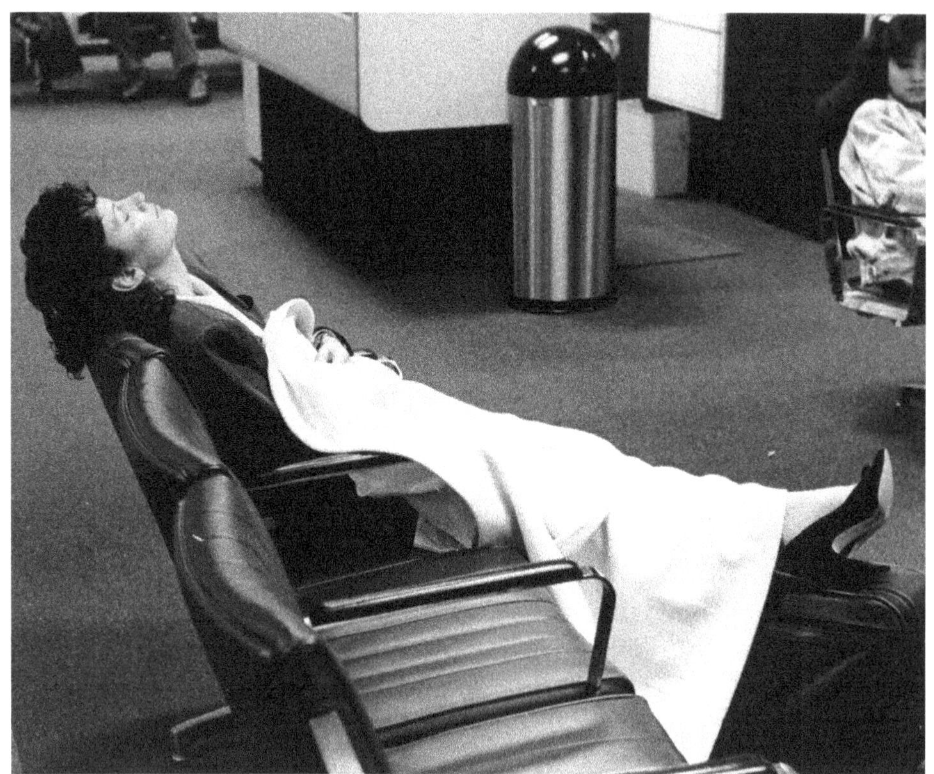

Sleeping Beauty
Atlanta

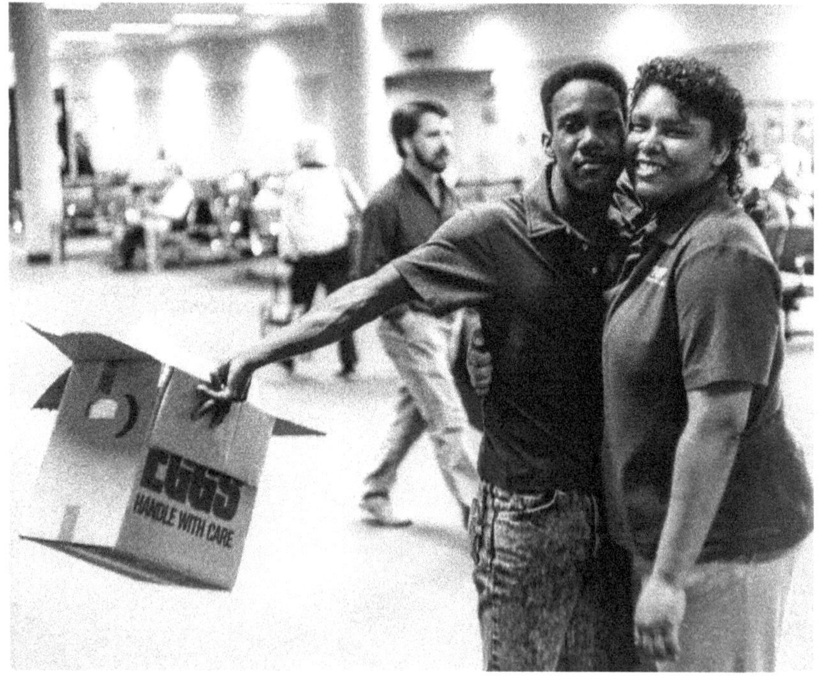

"Take my picture, it's my birthday!"
Atlanta

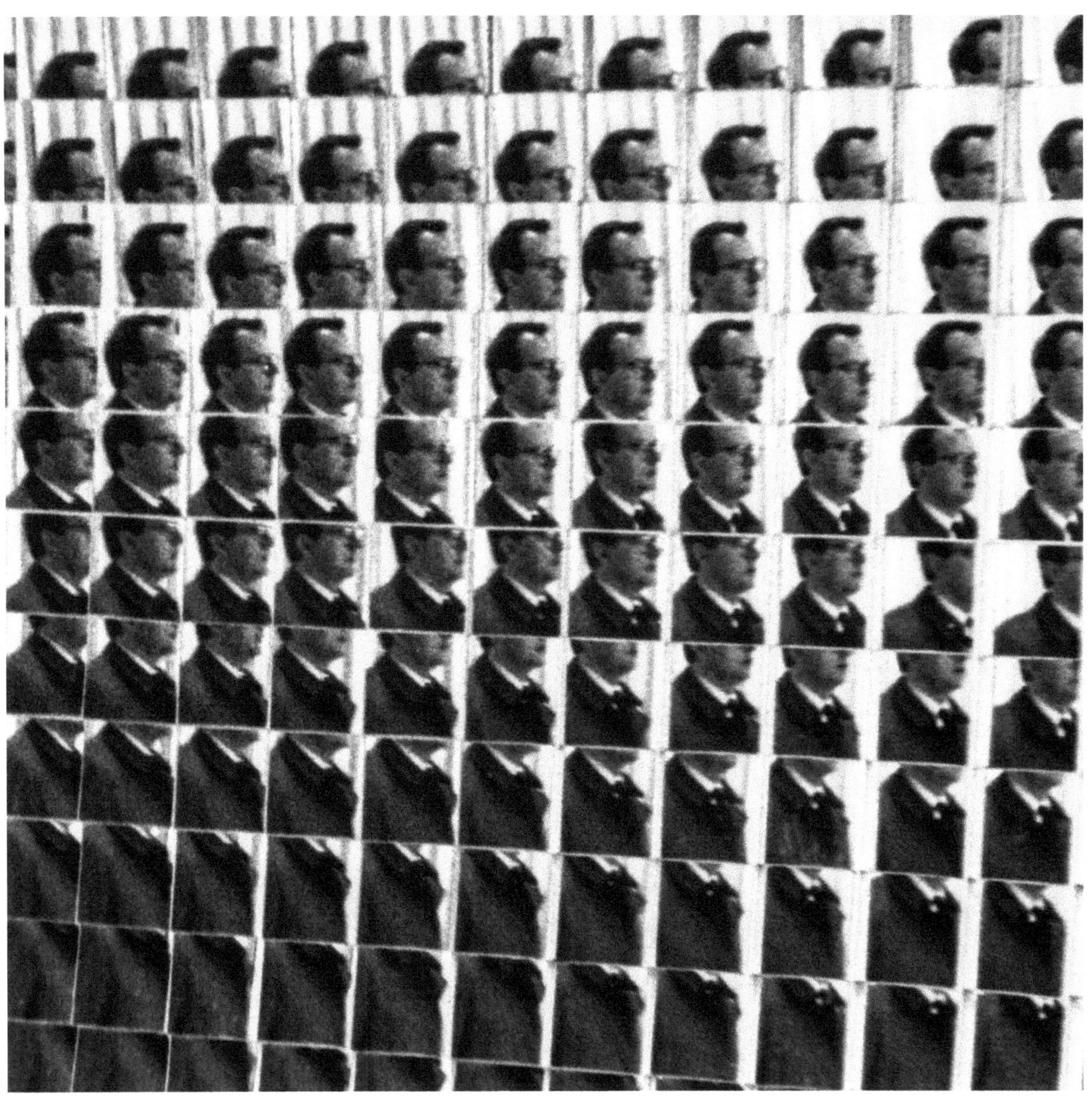

Boston Mirrors

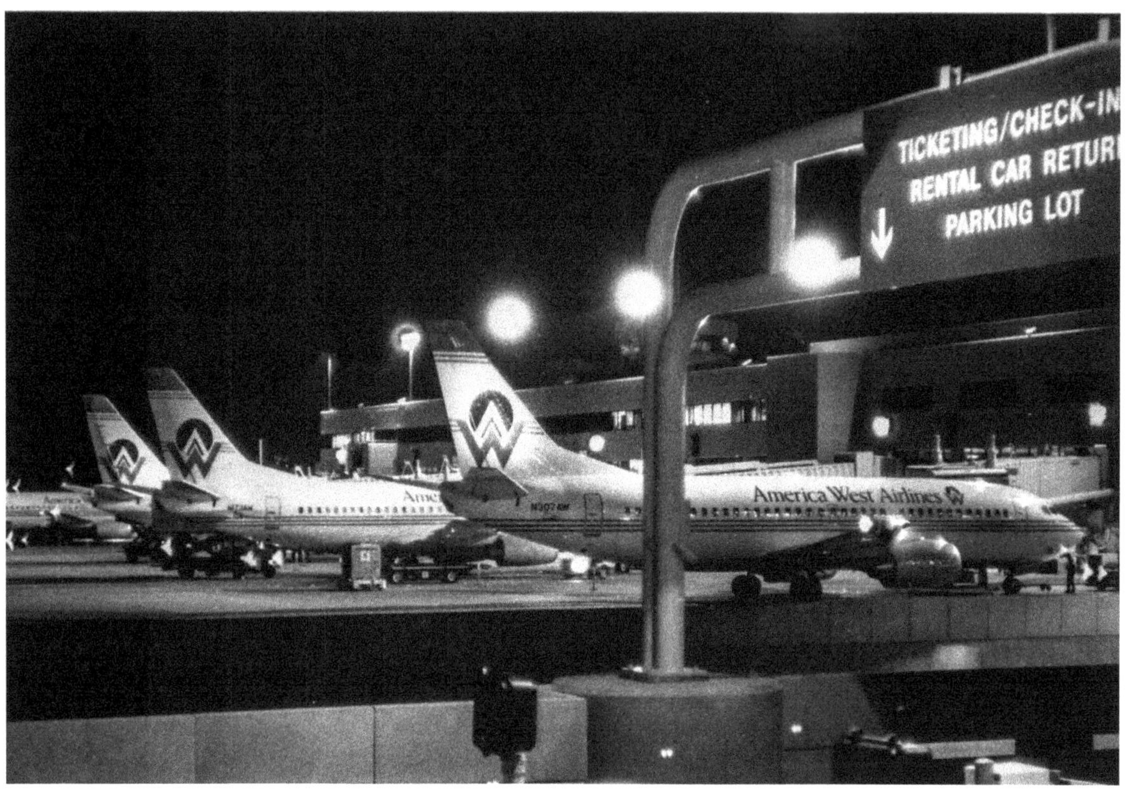

America West Airplanes

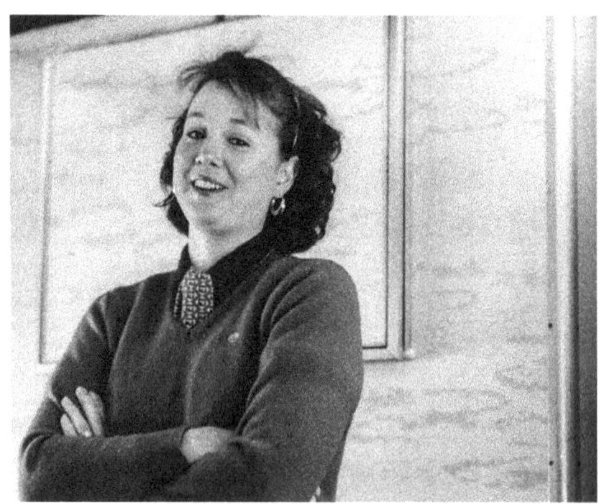

"You are not really taking my
picture, are you?"

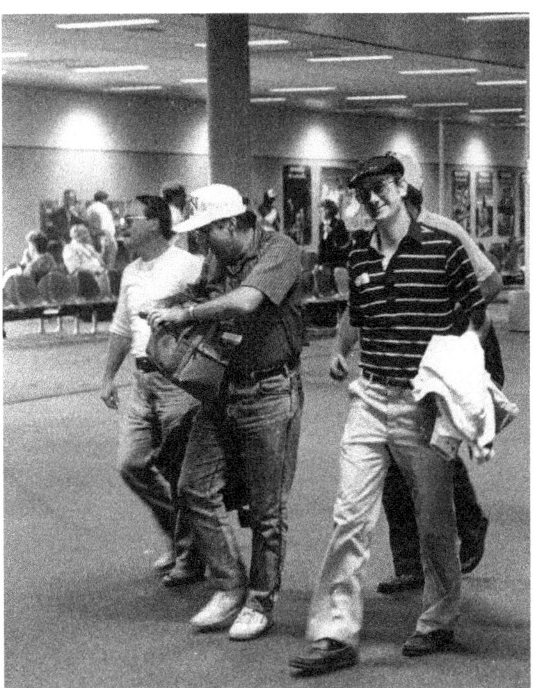

Atlanta Pleasure Trip

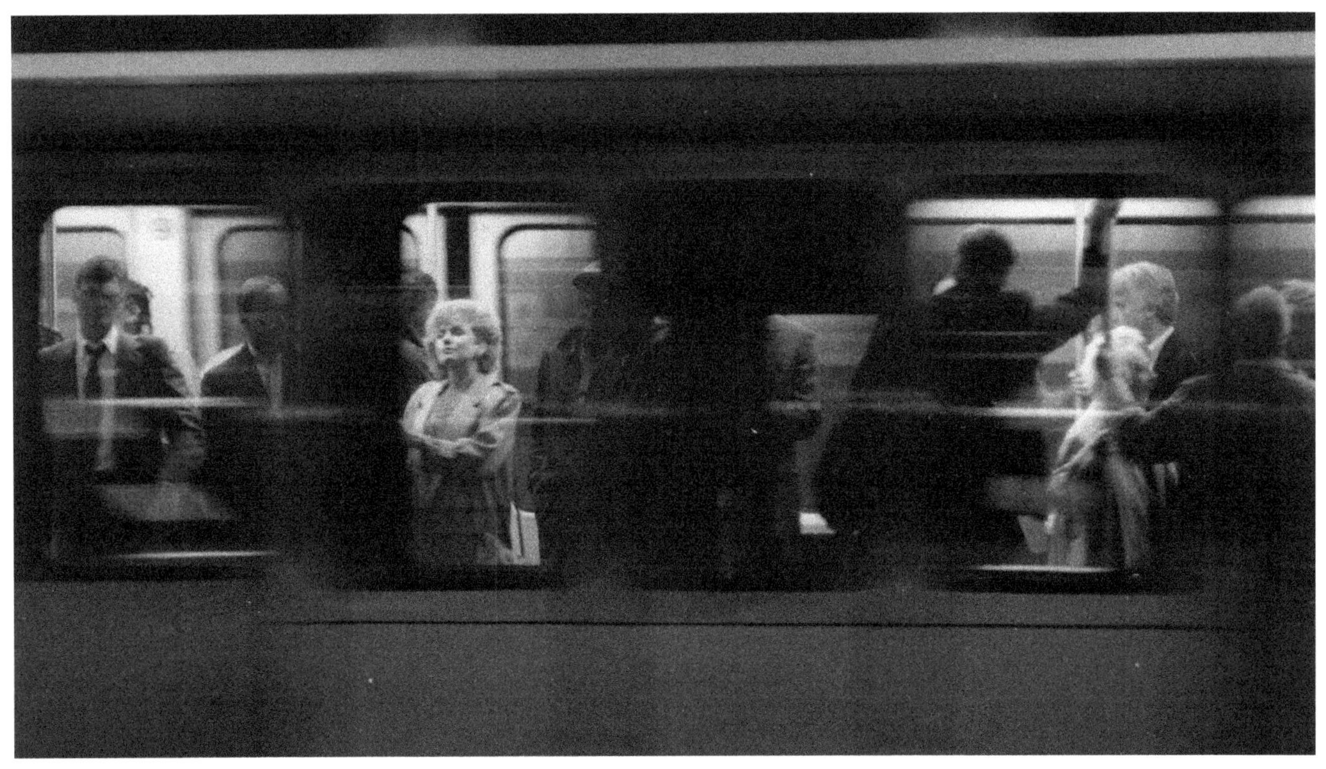

Train to the Gates
Atlanta

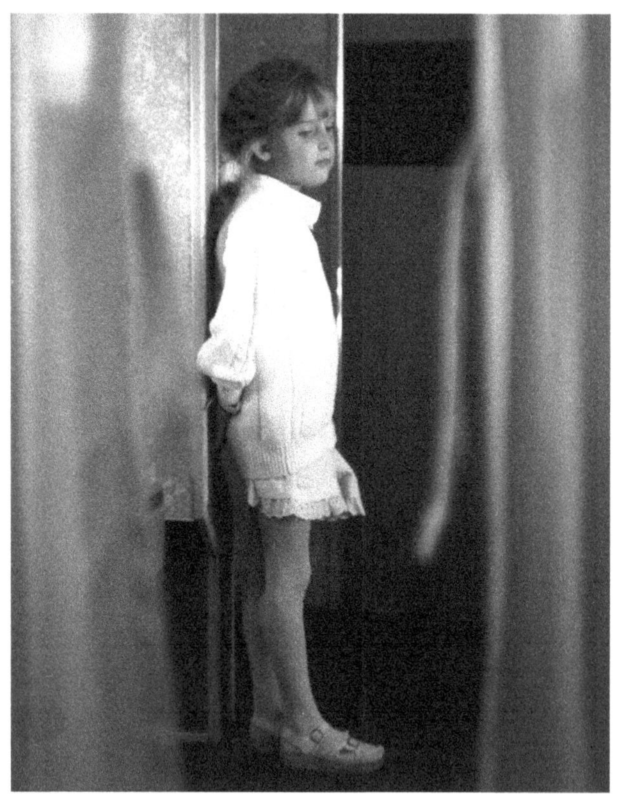

Waiting on the restroom, US Air Cleveland to Los Angeles

Flying home to Orlando after a visit to grandma in Indiana
Atlanta to Orlando

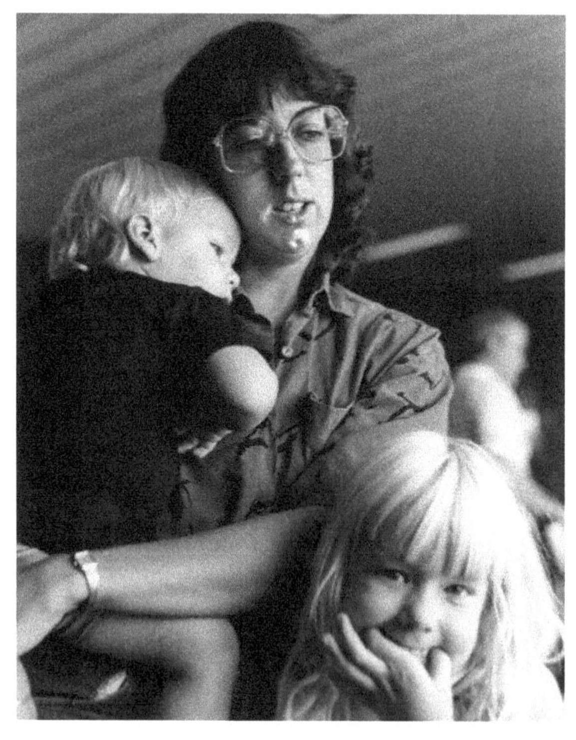

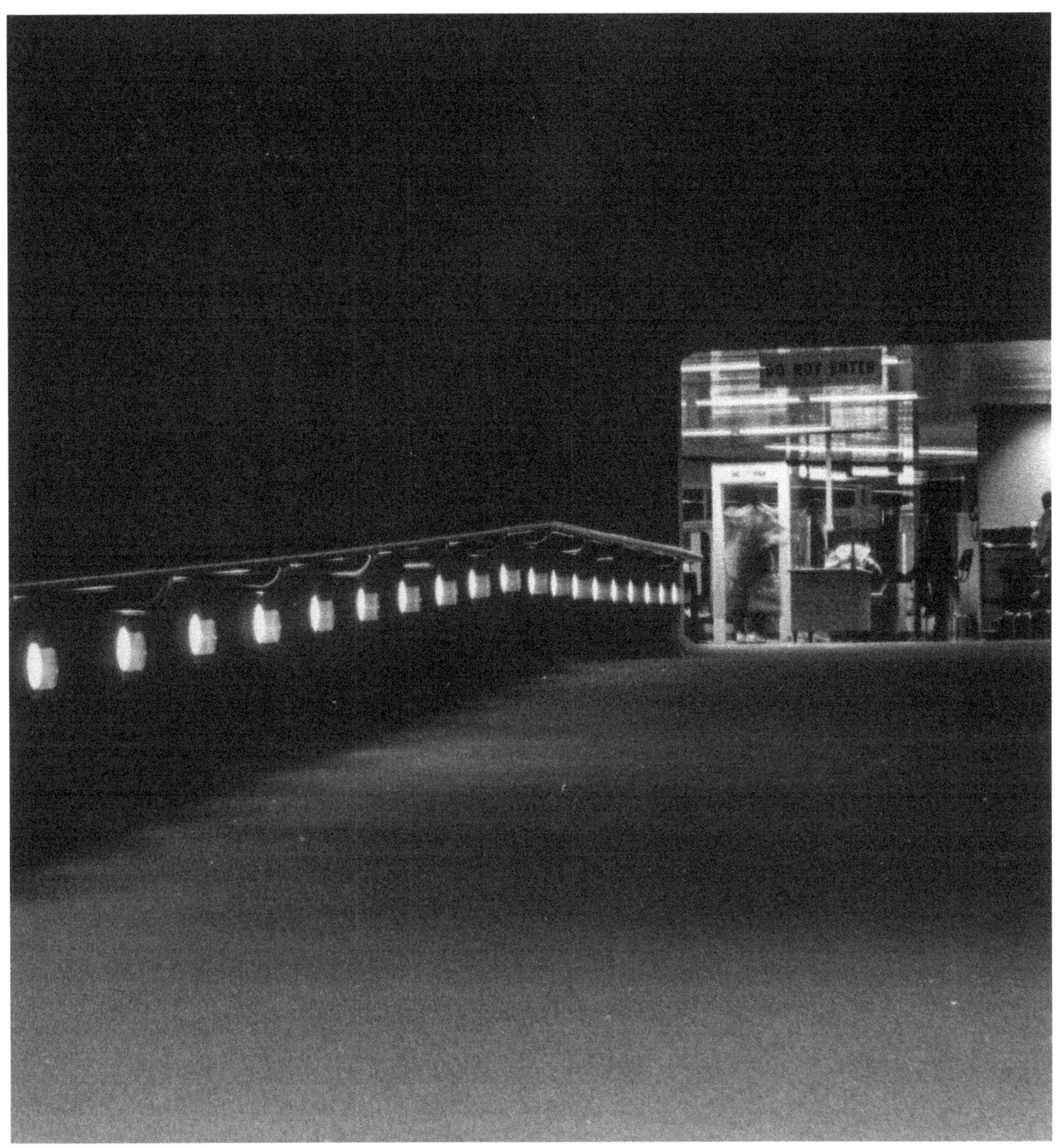

Security
St. Louis

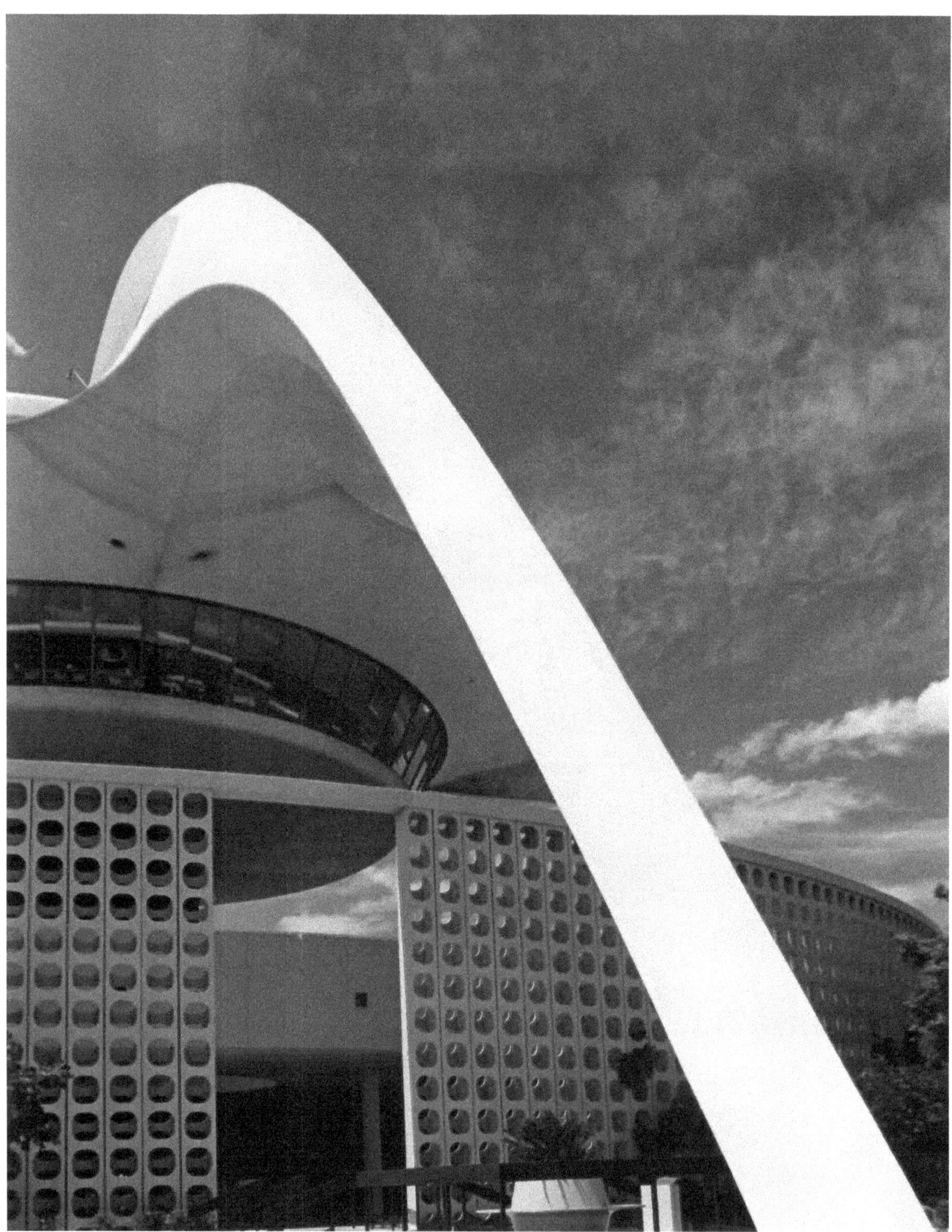

Theme Building Airport Restaurant
LAX Arch

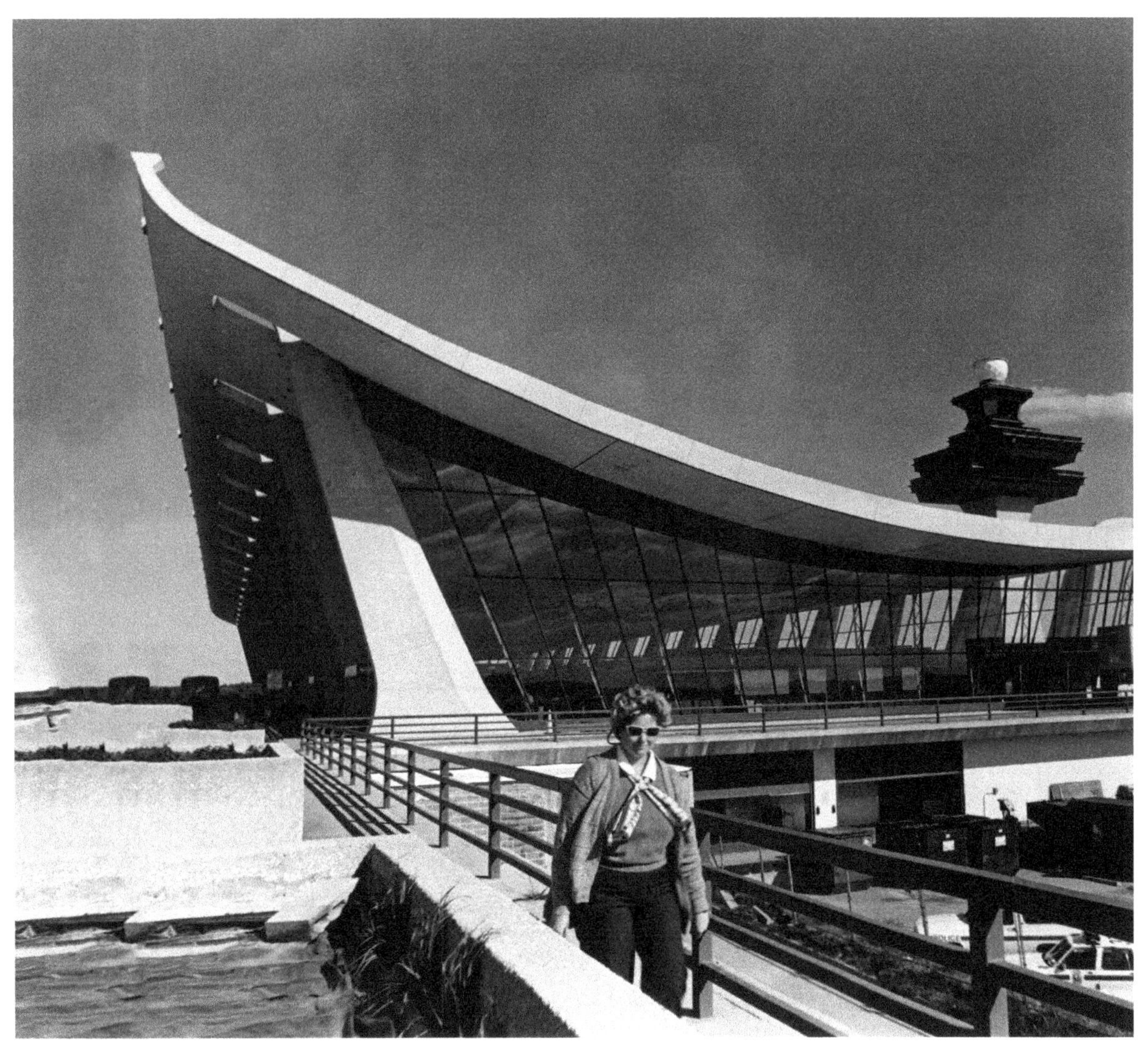

Dulles Airport

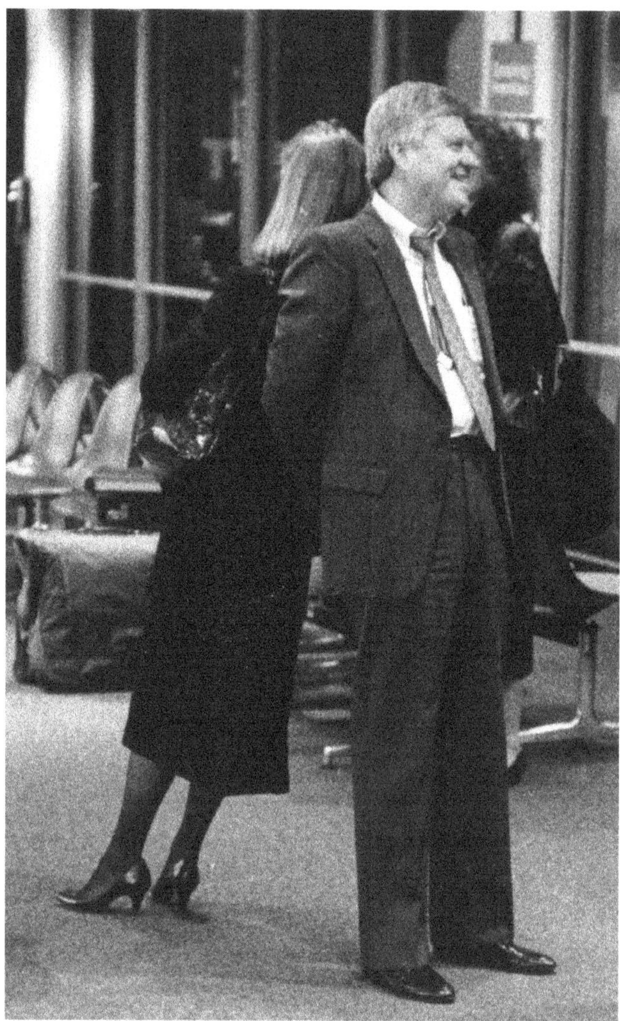

Clowning around
O'Hare

Skycap later asked me,
"Did you get my good side?"
Phoenix

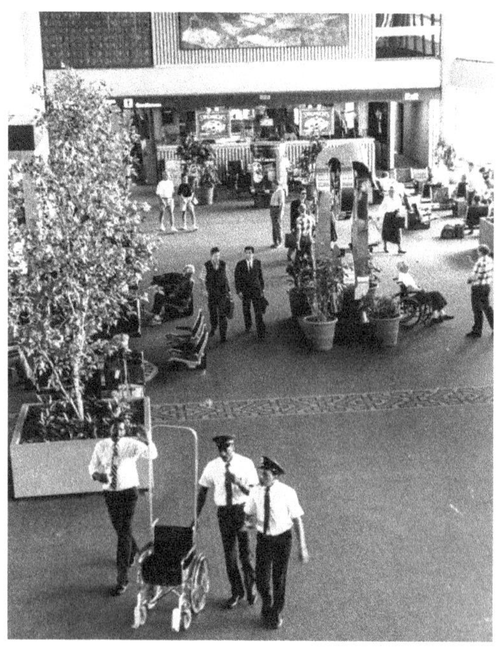

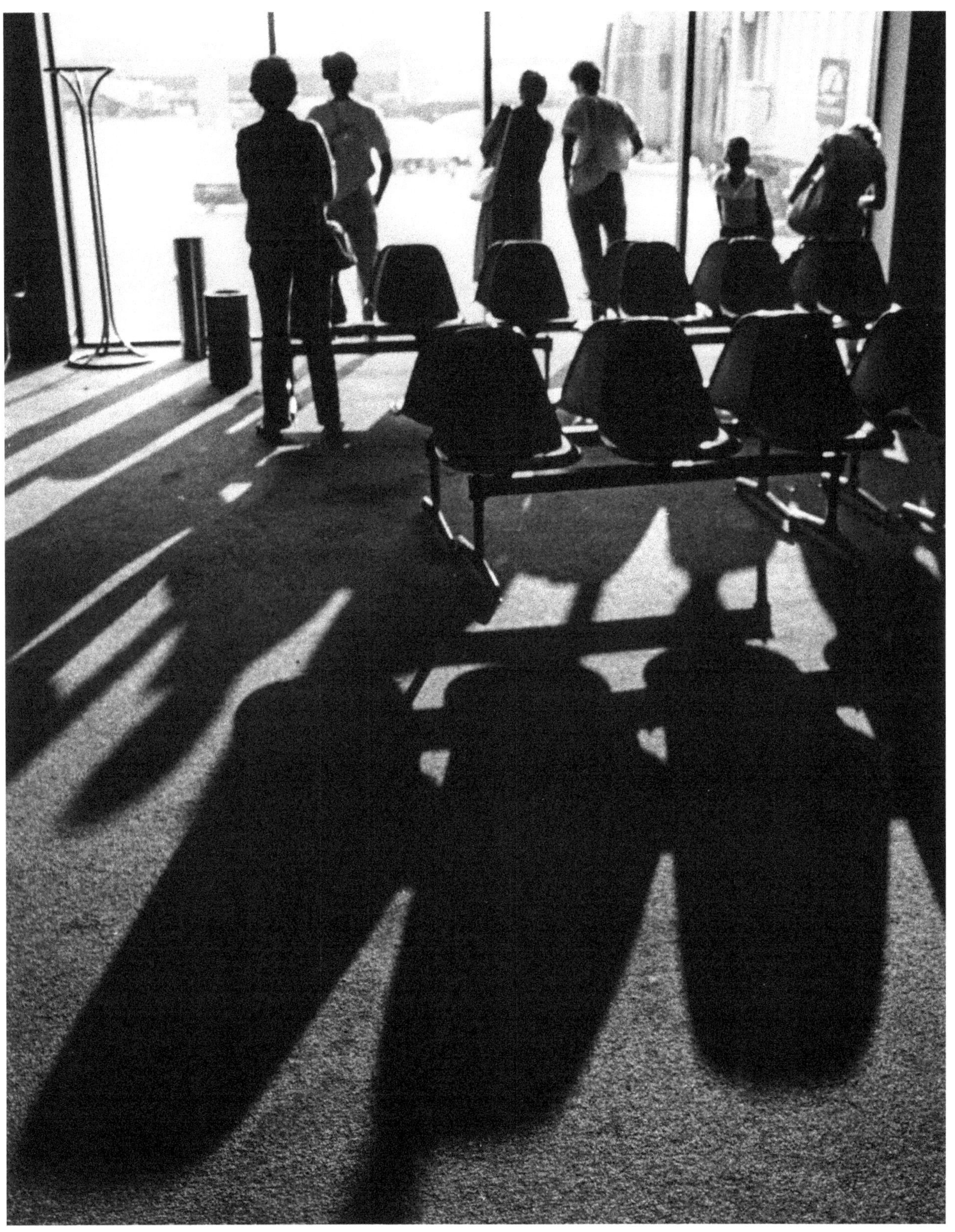

Atlanta Terminal

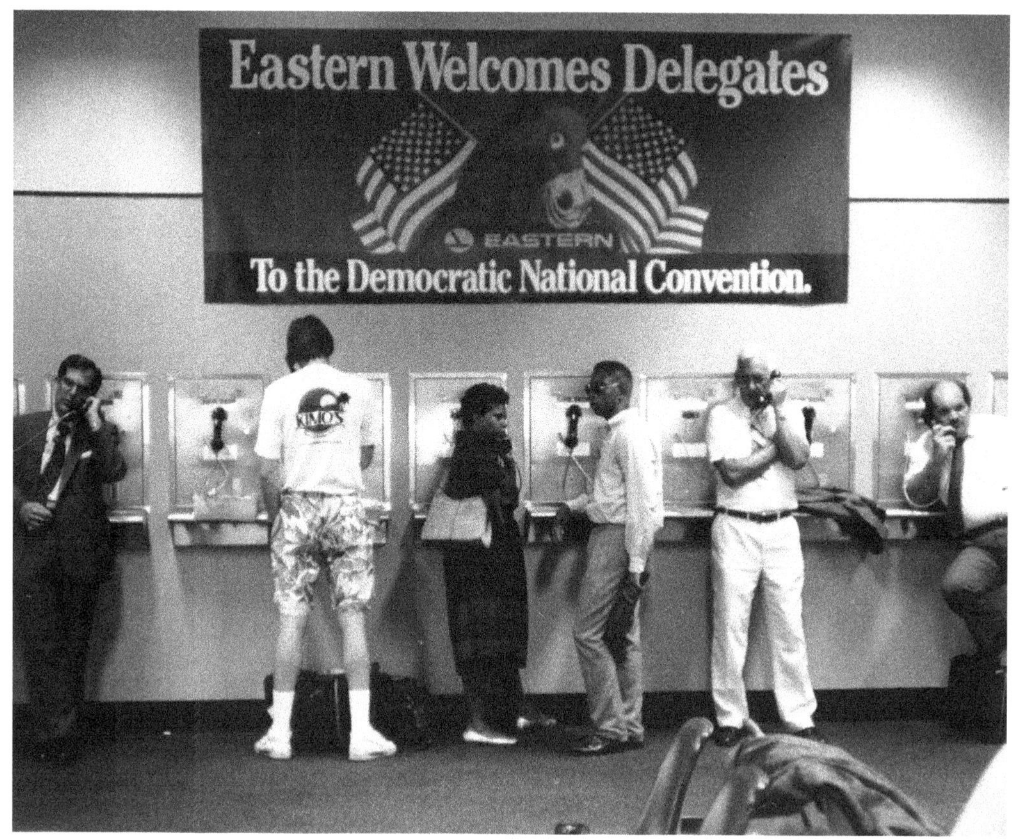

Eastern welcomes the Dems. Both losers in 1988

Hand signals
Atlanta

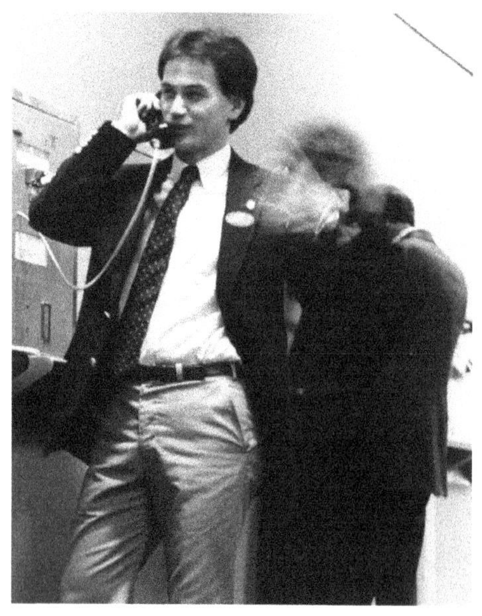

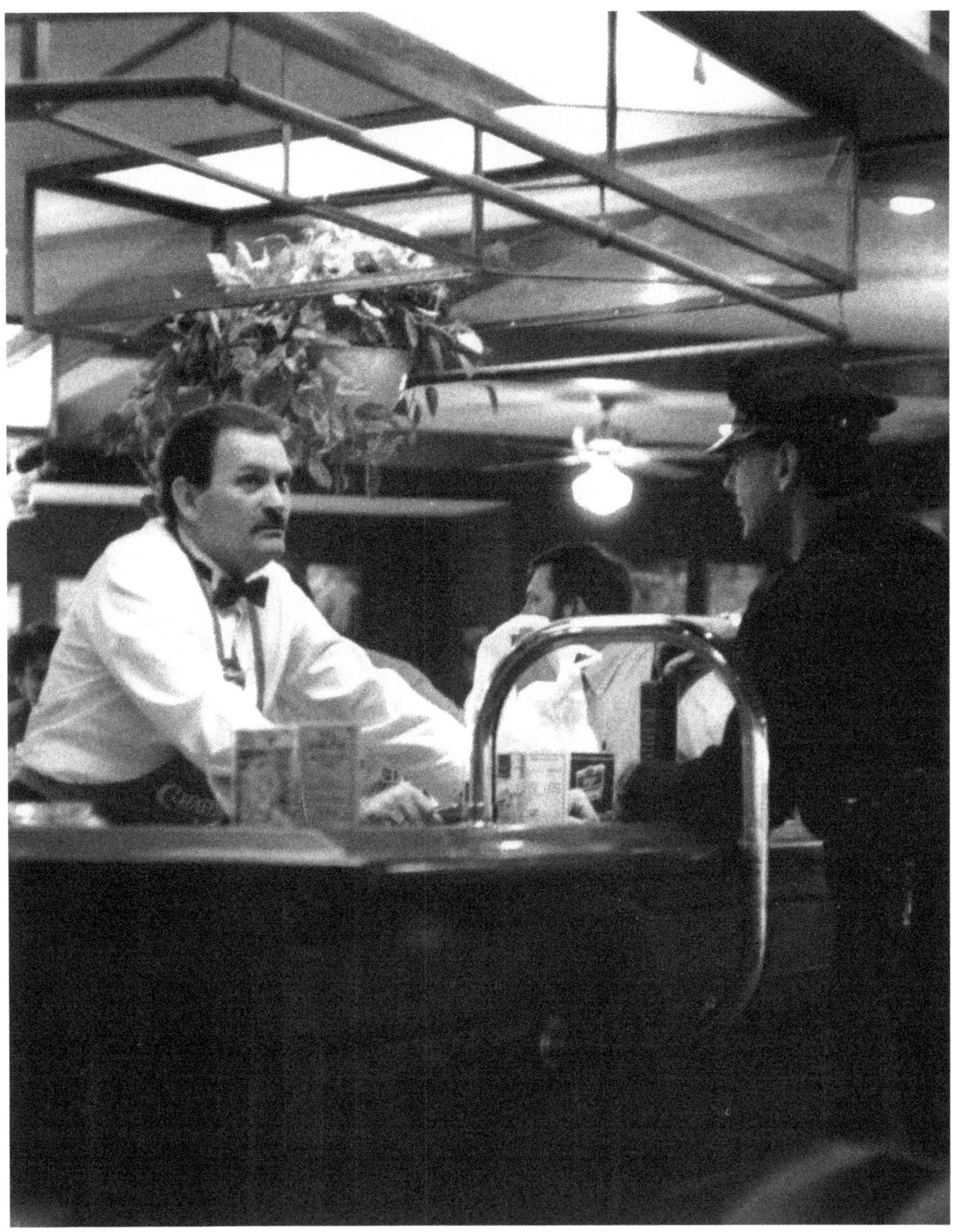

Bar, Logan Field

Boston

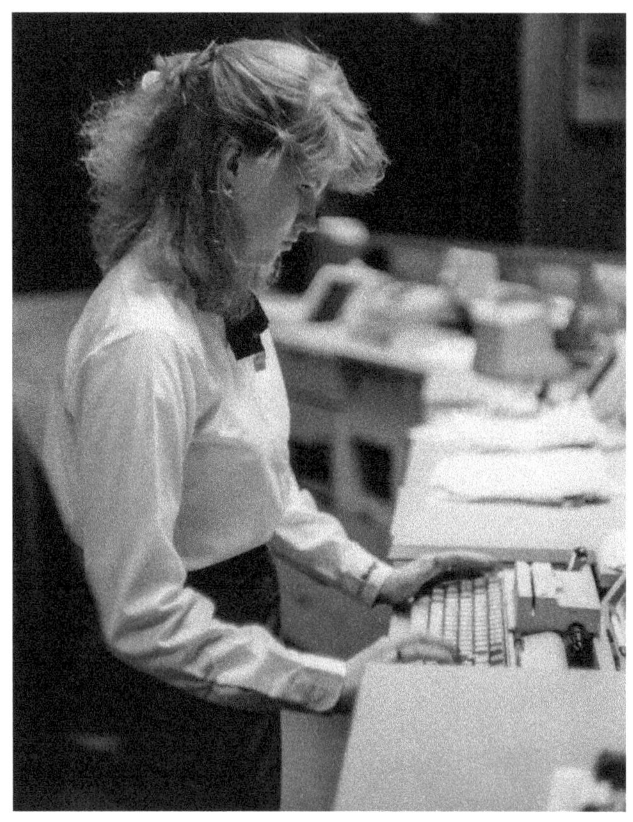

Car Rental
Dallas Fort Worth

Playtime
Atlanta

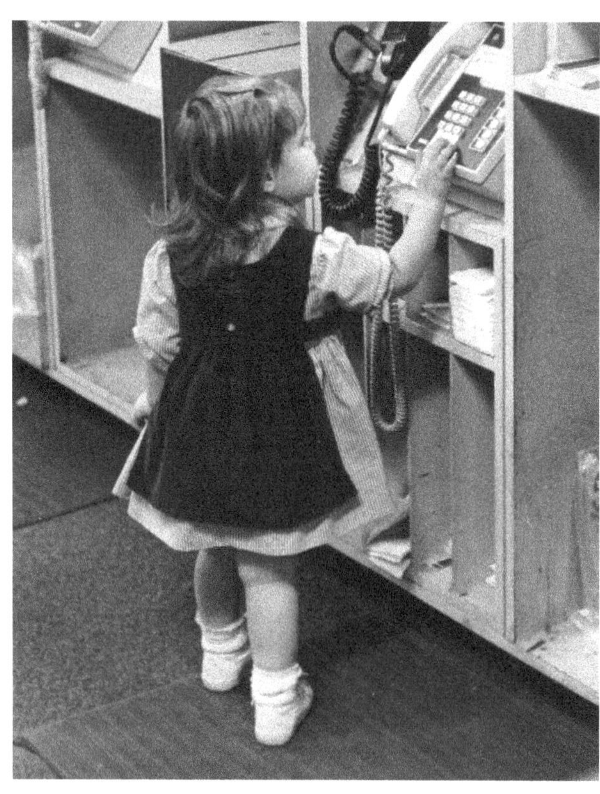

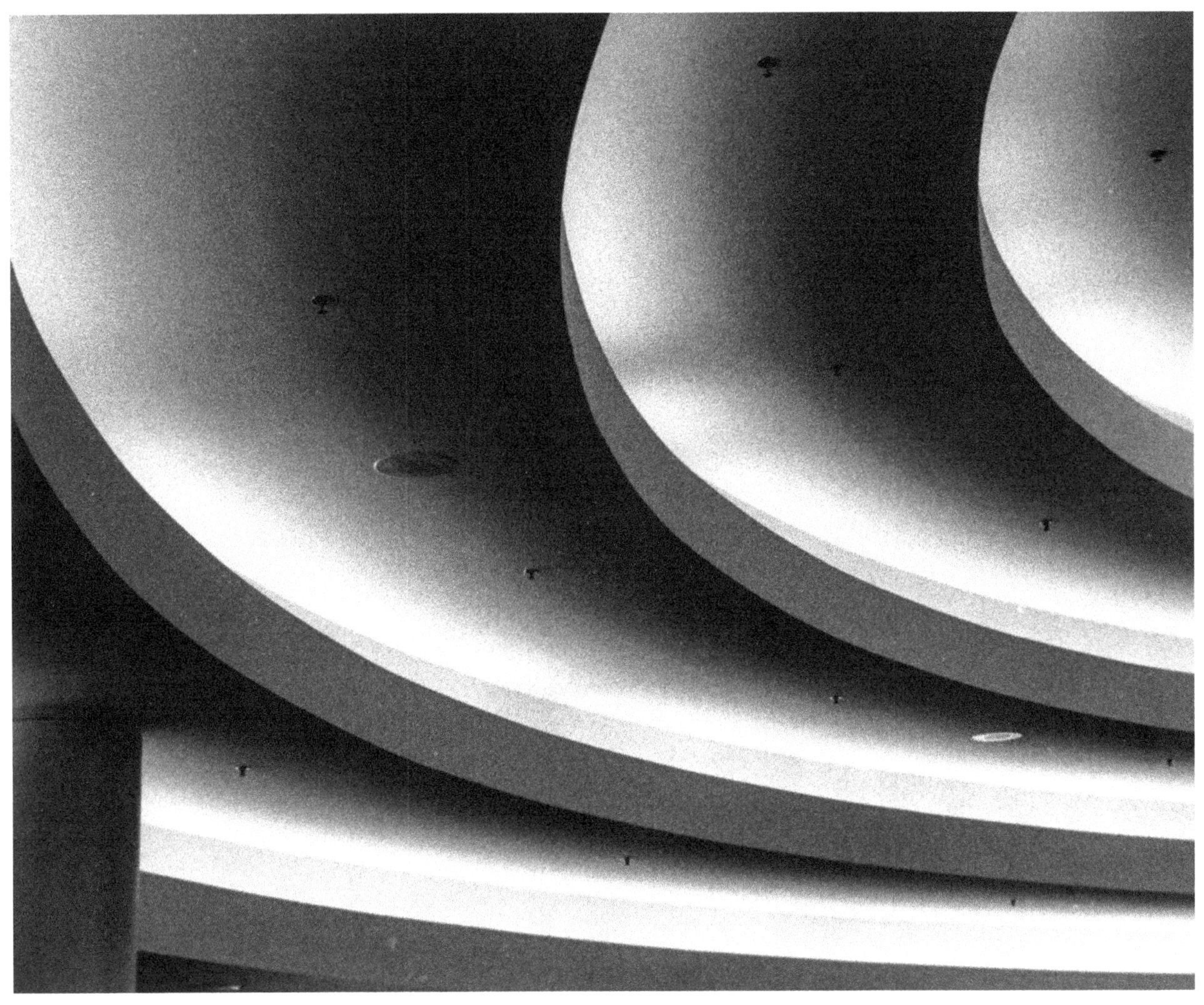

Ceiling

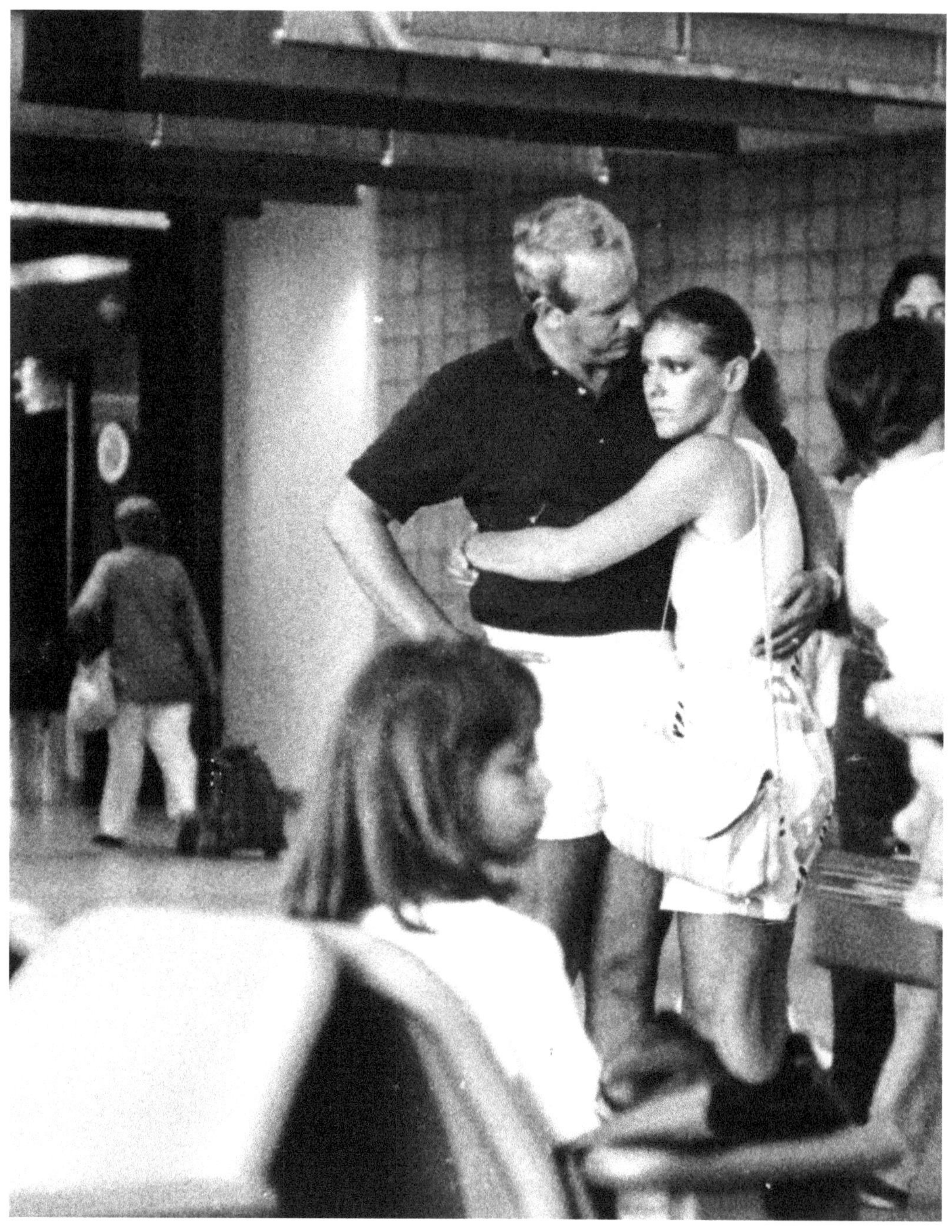

Apprehensive Arrival
Raleigh/Durham

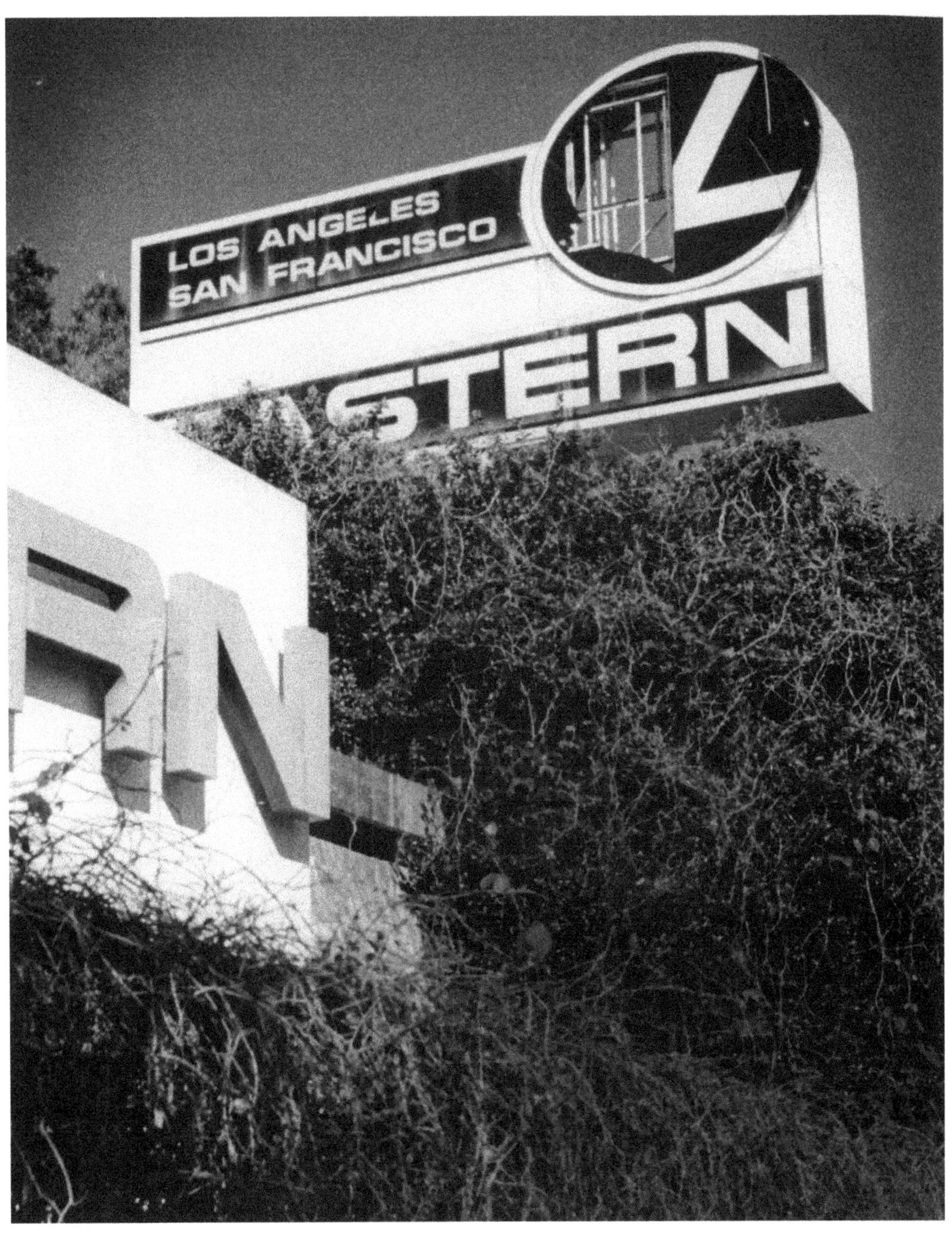

Post Mortem Eastern Airlines After the
corporate raiders sacked Eastern, service
began to decline. It resulted in "WHEAL"
club (We Hate Eastern Airlines)

About the Author

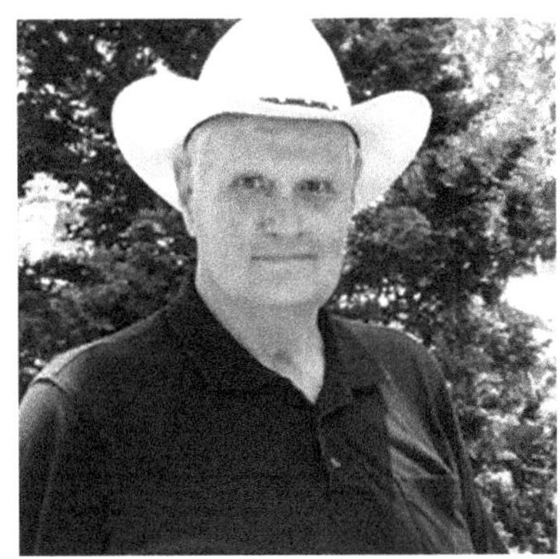

Eddie Morgan grew up with a darkroom in his home. His father was an internationally recognized photographer (Associate Royal Photographic Society) and some of his work was exhibited in the Smithsonian Institute.

Mr. Morgan has long pursued photography, switching from silver to electronic images in early 2000. He worked in the photo lab in the Manned Spacecraft Center in Houston, and for Eastman Kodak Company. He has sold numerous landscape images in art shows and sells stock photography.

More information about the book at **EddieMorgan.net**.

To learn about and purchase his landscape images check out **EddieMorgan.biz**.

Appendix
Index of Photographs

10 He was a Dean of the Florida Law School. He was currently running the Florida Department of Corrections under a court order due to overcrowding. 7-88

He was a professional crew member on racing yachts. He told me he hoped, one day, to use the MBA he earned at Harvard.   4-88

11 She was a marketing executive for a fast food franchisor. She was married to a TV producer, and this was the second time, by coincidence, I had set next to her on a flight. She was tired of the corporate grind and someday wanted to teach in a small college. 5-88

She was beautiful and looked too young to have been a communications consultant for AT&T for 18 years. 9-88

12 Front Cabin DC-9, Airplanes Avionics (the instruments used to fly the aircraft) were changing rapidly in the late '80s. The DC-9, a predecessor to the MD-80, had the older instruments and depended more on the pilot. A pilot for and L-1011 during this period, bragged that he could set the controls in Atlanta, and not touch them until after landing in Los Angeles. Even allowing for hyperbole, this was a major advance, and probably considered "crude" by today's standards. 6-88

13 Eastern emergency exit, 9-88

Food Service, Los Angeles to Atlanta, The most work a flight attendant does is food and beverage service. 3-90

14 Cool phone Atlanta, 4-88

Relaxing in the I-Club, 12-87

Nap Time Houston Hobby, 7-88

15 Bag Claim, Orange County, CA, 7-90

Generation Gap, Atlanta, 2-90

16 Window Cleaner, Atlanta, 3-90

Pre 9/11 Security, Atlanta, 9-88

17 People Mover, Dallas Love Field

18 She had been flying for 12 years. She had a daughter (19) and a son (9). Felt
    13 and 14 were the most difficult years. Washington National to Atlanta,
    3-90

    Shine man Business was slow today, but "you gotta do sumpin". He had lived
    in Chicago for 35 years, never been anywhere else. "Do they have busses in
    Atlanta?" O'Hare, 6-88

19 She had been flying for 17 years, and was worried about the financial
    stability of Eastern Airlines. "I just try to do my job the best I can every
    day." Samual Gompers, a founder of the American labor movement, was
    once quoted as saying "The cruelest condition management can impose on
    labor, is failure to make a profit." Atlanta to St. Louis, 2-90

    Shine Lady Management Student at North Texas State Dallas Ft. Worth,
    1-90

20 One was from Cleveland, one from Cincinnati, and one from Puerto Rico.
    They had just graduated from Marine boot camp that morning. When I
    asked them if I could take their picture, they all stood at attention. 7-88

21 I said, "Come on guys, boot camp is over." They all laughed for the second
    shot. 7-88

22 He was traveling to see his grandmother. He was a little scared. We talked
    about baseball cards, and when we got off the plane, he told me I was a nice
    guy. Atlanta to Dallas, 7-90

23 Snacks, Lexington to Atlanta, 2-89

    She was explaining to the first class passenger why he did not get a first class
    meal. 4-88

24 Shoe Shine Person, Dallas, 9-91

25 Clean up in Los Angeles, Los Angeles, 3-90

Men like this were invisible to the travelers, but without them, the system would not have worked. Atlanta, 7-88

26 Small Traveler, Big Bird, 5-88

Runner, Los Angeles, 12-90

27 Big Bird, Los Angeles, 5-91

28 Stand By, O'Hare, 5-88

Dead man walking Eastern Ticket Counter, Huntsville, AL, 5-88

29 Long Flight, Los Angeles to Atlanta, 4-88

30 By the 1980's the life of the crew was long days with endless check ins. Flight Crew check in, hotel, Huntsville, AL, 5-88

Night Shift, Los Angeles, 8-88

31 American Airlines Plane Tail

32 He was the son of a missionary and attended Wheaton Bible College. He had been a missionary himself (France) and was now with a software company. He trains Doctors on how the use their software.
Atlanta to Ft. Lauderdale FL, 3-90

She had been a business consultant in the medical field for 18 years. She entered the field after she was turned down for medical school. She told me that she traveled a lot, frequently worked for eighteen hours per day when she was on the road. She shared that her business life left little time for personal life and no time to have a family.
Atlanta to Los Angeles, 3-91

33 She was flying to California for Christmas with her family. She and her husband were separated, and she still loved him. He had a substance abuse problem, and she was not going to go back with him until he dealt with it. Cleveland to Boston, 12-90

He was a computer sales executive who had transferred to California from the Midwest. His family was "adjusting." 7-91

34 Sculpture, Kids Playing, Miami

35   Family boarding Atlanta to Houston, 9-88

Carry on, San Juan Puerto Rico "All carry on must be able to fit in the overhead compartment or under the seat in front of you." 8-88

36   She was just starting a 6 day trip. Based in Atlanta, she had a 15 month old son, who missed her when she was gone. She left before he woke up for her trips, to avoid tears (hers and his). Atlanta to Chicago, 6-88

New flight attendant Houston to Atlanta, 12-89

37   Eastern flight attendents going to work In the early years, it was considered a "glamorous" job. The pay was relatively high (for a young female, which was the only people they hired at the time) and they got to travel. They were hired for their looks and their personality. 10-90

Although it was nowhere near as common as assumed, there was always an assumption that there were affairs between the pilots (almost all male in the early days) and flight attendants. The old joke was a pilot, thinking he was on a private communication, said "Beautiful, bring me some of your hot coffee and your hot love," which was heard by the entire plane. As the flight attendant rushed to the flight deck to inform him that is was being broadcast, someone shouted "Hey Beautiful, you forgot the coffee." Flight deck service Atlanta to St. Louis, 2-90

38   Small mother, big airportAtlanta airport, 3-90

Washington National, 2-90

39   Cincinnati People Mover, 2-89

40   She was from Yorkshire, England, and had married a U. S. Marine Sergeant. She moved to Atlanta in 9-89, and was very homesick, but couldn't go home until 9-90. Atlanta to Los Angeles, 3-90

"I take such a bad picture" Atlanta Ionosphere Club, 3-90

41   She had been a recovery room nurse since the divorce (5 years ago) and was

worried about the health care problems facing the country.
Los Angeles to Atlanta, 3-90

As the industry matured, their pay was reduced to the point where there was a two tiered system in most airlines, with some of the younger hires paid as though it was a "part time" job, since they did not work a standard 40 hour week. Take off, Atlanta to St. Louis, 2-90

42 Corridor, Washington National, 2-90

43 No solicitation, just waiting on an arriving passenger, 3-90

Good Night, Miami, 9-90

44 Phoenix Parking, 4-91

45 New Orleans Superdome Convention, 5-90

French Quarter, Iron Work, 10-89

46 O'Hare Business conference, 5-88

So this guy came into the bar and said to the bartender, "What's the strongest thing you got back there". Without batting an eye, the bartender said, "I don't know, try the coffee." Bar, Red Lion Inn, Costa Mesa, CA, 7-90

47 Hampton Inn, Schaumburg, IL, 7-88

48 Mannequins in the Gift Shop, DFW Gift Shop, 2-90

Pool, Holiday Inn, Paducah KY, 6-88

49 Marriott Marquis, New York, 12-87

50 Sleeping Beauty, Atlanta, 1-90

"Take my picture, it's my birthday!" Atlanta, 3-90

51 Boston Mirrors, 2-91

America West Airplanes

52 "You are not really taking my picture, are you?" 4-88

53 Train to the Gates, Atlanta, 10-88

Atlanta Pleasure Trip, 7-89

54 Flying home to Orlando after a visit to grandma in Indiana
Atlanta to Orlando, 8-88

Waiting on the restroom. US Air, Cleveland to Los Angeles, 12-90

55 Security, St. Louis, 2-90

56 Theme Building Airport Restaurant, LAX Arch, 8-90

57 Dulles Airport, 8-90

58 Skycap later asked me, "Did you get my good side?" Phoenix, 4-90

Clowning around, O'Hare, 1989

59 Atlanta Terminal

60 Eastern welcomes the Dems, Both losers in 1988, 7-88

Hand signals, Atlanta, 9-88

61 Bar, Logan Field, Boston, 12-90

62 Car Rental, Dallas Fort Worth, 6-88

Playtime, Atlanta, 4-88

63 Ceiling

64 Apprehensive Arrival, Raleigh/Durham, 8-88

65 Post Mortem Eastern Airlines After the corporate raiders sacked Eastern,
service began to decline. It resulted in "WHEAL" club (We Hate Eastern
Airlines)

CPSIA information can be obtained
at www.ICGtesting.com
Printed in the USA
LVHW01s0924160418
573592LV00005B/5/P